Living the Intersection

LIVING THE INTERSECTION
Womanism and Afrocentrism
✦✦✦✦✦✦✦ in Theology ✦✦✦✦✦✦✦

Cheryl J. Sanders
Editor

FORTRESS PRESS
Minneapolis

LIVING THE INTERSECTION
Womanism and Afrocentrism in Theology

Library of Congress Cataloging-in-Publication Data

Living the intersection : womanism and Afrocentrism in theology /
    Cheryl J. Sanders, editor.
       p.   cm.
    Includes bibliographical references.
    ISBN 0-8006-2852-7
    1. Womanist theology.   2. Afrocentrism—Religious aspects—
Christianity.   I. Sanders, Cheryl Jeanne.
    BT83.9.L58   1995
    230′.082—dc20   94-33746
                                                                   CIP

The paper used in this publication meets the minimum requirements of
American National Standard for Information Sciences—Permanence of
Paper for Printed Library Materials, ANSI Z329.48-1984.   ∞™

Manufactured in U.S.A.   AF 1–2852

99   98   97   96   95   1   2   3   4   5   6   7   8   9   10

Contents

Contributors 7

Introduction 9
Kelly Brown Douglas and *Cheryl J. Sanders*

Part One **Experience**

1. We Have a Beautiful Mother:
Womanist Musings on the Afrocentric Idea 21
Cheryl Townsend Gilkes

2. Afrocentrism and Male-Female Relations
in Church and Society 43
Delores S. Williams

3. A Womanist Response to the Afrocentric Idea:
Jarena Lee, Womanist Preacher 57
Lorine L. Cummings

4. To Reflect the Image of God:
A Womanist Perspective on Right Relationship 67
Kelly Brown Douglas

Part Two **Interpretation**

5. Slavery as a Sacred Text: Witnessing in *Dessa Rose* 81
Deborah E. McDowell

6.   Living in the Intersection of Womanism
      and Afrocentrism: Black Women Writers   *105*
      Youtha C. Hardman-Cromwell

7.   Black Women in Biblical Perspective:
      Resistance, Affirmation, and Empowerment   *121*
      Cheryl J. Sanders

      Part Three   **Learning**

8.   Teaching Womanist Theology   *147*
      Kelly Brown Douglas

9.   Afrocentric and Womanist Approaches
      to Theological Education   *157*
      Cheryl J. Sanders

Notes   177

Index   191

Contributors

Lorine L. Cummings is pastor and founder of the Pentecostal Baptist Church in Baltimore, Maryland. She formerly served as associate minister at New Psalmist Baptist Church in Baltimore. A professional social worker since 1977, she is supervisor of adult services at the Baltimore County Department of Social Services.

Kelly Brown Douglas is Associate Professor of Theology at the Howard University School of Divinity, and is an Episcopal priest. She is the author of *The Black Christ*, a study in womanist Christology.

Cheryl Townsend Gilkes is MacArthur Associate Professor of African-American Studies and Sociology at Colby College, Waterville, Maine, and Associate Minister of the Union Baptist Church, Cambridge, Massachusetts. Her research centers on culture and community in African American religious experience, on which she has published in the *Journal of Religious Thought, Journal of Feminist Studies in Religion, Signs*, and in the volume *A Troubling in My Soul*.

Youtha C. Hardman-Cromwell is Visiting Associate Professor of Pastoral Theology at the Howard University School of Divinity, Washington, D.C. She is a ministry consultant and formerly was pastor of the Woodlawn United Methodist Church in Alexandria, Virginia.

Deborah E. McDowell is Professor of English at the University of Virginia, Charlottesville. She is author of *"The Changing Same": Studies in Fiction by Black Women* (Indiana University Press, 1991) and co-editor of *Slavery and the Literary Imagination* (Johns Hopkins Univ. Press, 1989).

Cheryl J. Sanders is Associate Professor of Christian Ethics at the Howard University School of Divinity. She is Associate Pastor for Leadership Development at Third Street Church of God in Washington, D.C., and is the author of a history of that congregation, *How Firm a Foundation*.

Delores S. Williams is Associate Professor of Theology and Culture at Union Theological Seminary, New York. She is author of *Sisters in the Wilderness: The Challenge of Womanist God-Talk* (Orbis Books, 1993).

Introduction

◆◆◆◆◆◆◆◆◆◆◆◆◆◆◆◆◆◆◆◆◆◆◆◆◆◆◆◆◆◆◆◆◆

Kelly Brown Douglas and Cheryl J. Sanders

Womanism and Afrocentricity are two exciting perspectives that have recently emerged in the African American community. African American women have given birth to the womanist idea. In essence, a womanist is a black feminist who is committed to the survival and wholeness of entire people, male and female.[1] While the term *womanist* was coined by Pulitzer Prize–winning novelist Alice Walker in her 1983 volume, *In Search of Our Mothers' Gardens*, its usage now goes beyond her definition. African American women have adopted the term as a symbol of their experience. *Womanist* signals an appreciation for the richness, complexity, uniqueness, and struggle involved in being black and female in a society that is hostile to both blackness and womanhood.

African American males have taken the lead in articulating the Afrocentric concept. Molefi Kete Asante, however, has brought the term to prominence and clarified its meaning. In his text *Afrocentricity*, Asante defines Afrocentricity as "the belief in the centrality of Africans in post-modern history."[2] He delineates the implications of Afrocentric belief for the way African Americans negotiate life in a white racist society. The

Afrocentric idea demonstrates the vitality of African American culture and history, as well as the African heritage. It excavates the African past in an effort to free African Americans from an oppressive Eurocentric consciousness and to create for them a new, African-centered way of thinking and acting. While the term certainly owes its breadth and depth to Asante, it has come to voice in the African American community as a profound recognition of the richness, significance, and uniqueness of the African American cultural heritage in a society that devalues that heritage.

The terms *womanist* and *womanism* are used in this volume to refer to the vantage point of those who share Alice Walker's perspective on the collective experience and struggles of African American women. The Afrocentric nomenclature includes several terms derived from the work of Molefi Asante—*Afrocentric, Afrocentricity, Afrocentricism,* and *Afrocentrism.* Although the terms *Afrocentricism* and *Afrocentrism* do not appear in Asante's own writings, in this collection of essays they are used interchangeably with Asante's preferred term, *Afrocentricity.*

At first glance, the womanist and Afrocentric perspectives bear striking similarities to each other. Both have emerged as parts of an oppressed people's culture of resistance. Womanist scholarship gives expression to African American women's efforts—political, cultural, emotional, psychological, spiritual—to resist the "interlocking system"[3] of multiple oppression, i.e., racism, sexism, and classism, that would thwart the life and well-being of African American women and men as well as girls and boys. The womanist perspective, therefore, involves mining the culture and history of African American women in an effort to forge a way of living that fosters life and wholeness for the African American community.

Although Asante asserts that "both male and female scholars must properly examine the roles women have played in liberating Africans and others from oppression, resisting the imposition of sexist repression and subjugation, and exercising economic and political authority,"[4] the compatibility of womanist and Afrocentric perspectives has become a source of concern. While African American women clearly live in the intersection between the two viewpoints, being at once African American and female, the receptivity of Afrocentricity to womanist concerns is not readily apparent. Womanist scholars have attested to the prevalence of Afrocentric ways of knowing and acting in African American women's quest for survival, wholeness, and liberation. Yet they have variously questioned whether Afrocentrism, as developed by contemporary male scholars, is a perspective that mitigates African American women's personhood and freedom. This text is a collective effort undertaken by African American women scholars in the field of religion to explore the intricate relationship between Afrocentric and womanist perspectives.

Several reasons compel African American theologians and religious scholars to take such a keen interest in Afrocentrism and womanism. First is the fact that religion has played a key role in the African American experience historically. Thus, potentially every new intellectual development bears some relationship with the sacred worldview manifested in black religious communities. Clearly, both Molefi Asante and Alice Walker have had formative experiences in the black church that give substance and context to much of their writing. The African American womanist theologians are endeavoring to foster a mutually enriching dialogue between these and other African American intellectuals and black religious folk. Second, the premier paradigm for interpretation within the black community historically has been the prophetic proclamation of the black preacher. The pervasive presence of religion and spirituality in black culture has expanded the scope of this interpretive work to include a wide array of ideas and impulses. Most of the African American womanist scholars who are preachers are profoundly sensitive to the cultural concerns of black people and are engaged in a twofold interpretive task: to interpret the significance of Afrocentric and womanist ideas in ways that people in the churches and community can understand, on the one hand, and to give expression to the distinctive ideas emerging from African American life using the language, structures, and vehicles of the academy, on the other. This interpretive role is closely related to a third factor relating African American religious scholars to Afrocentrism and womanism, namely, the mandate to teach. Not only is this a manifestation of the desire to include reflections on race and gender in the content of what is taught; it also indicates the extent to which African American women teaching in the seminaries, universities, and churches have themselves been taught by Asante and Walker.

Most of these chapters were written in response to a call for creative engagement of Afrocentric and womanist thought at the Howard University School of Divinity. Its two-year faculty scholarship development project was funded by the Lilly Foundation and was designed to explore the implications of the Afrocentric idea for black theological education. Related to this project were two events: (1) a panel of theological faculty and student papers on "Womanist Responses to the Afrocentric Idea," presented during the 1992 Annual Meeting of the American Academy of Religion and Society of Biblical Literature, Mid-Atlantic Region in Washington, D.C.; and (2) the 1992 Feminine in Religious Traditions Lecture Series at the Howard University School of Divinity, with a focus on the same theme. The essays by Youtha C. Hardman-Cromwell, Lorine L. Cummings, Cheryl Townsend Gilkes, Cheryl J. Sanders, and Delores S. Williams were originally presented or developed as part of this project. A second formative source of these documents was a conference convened at Princeton

Theological Seminary in 1988, also funded by the Lilly Foundation, which sought to explore the implications of African American women's literature for the field of hermeneutics in religious and theological studies. Deborah E. McDowell presented her essay at the Princeton conference. Douglas's essay on womanist relationships was originally delivered at the 1993 Annual Meeting of the American Academy of Religion in Washington, D.C., as a part of a panel of womanist and black male theologians discussing male and female relationships.

Part One of *Living the Intersection* is titled "Experience" because experience is the starting point for the scholarly reflection of African American women engaged in the study of religion and society. Each author in this section attempts to describe and evaluate the experience of women who "live the intersection" of African and female identity in the United States. In her essay, "We Have a Beautiful Mother: Womanist Musings on the Afrocentric Idea," Cheryl Townsend Gilkes offers a rich collection of personal reflections. Through these reflections she first suggests that Afrocentric concerns were a part of African American life long before the term *Afrocentrism* was coined. Gilkes's musings then lead her to offer certain caveats concerning the contemporary Afrocentric movement. She warns, for instance, that while Afrocentrism is "an important public challenge to white supremacist myths and . . . intellectual justifications," its proponents must be careful not to lead the African American community into ideological bondage. Gilkes concludes her reflections by exploring her contention that womanist thought is Afrocentric, though all thinking about Afrocentrism is not womanist.

Delores S. Williams is more harsh in her criticisms of Afrocentrism as it involves African American women. Her chapter, "Afrocentrism and Male-Female Relations in Church and Society" argues that Afrocentrism, as developed by

Asante, is "woman-exclusive while it pretends to be inclusive of all black people." She shows how women are invisible in Afrocentrism until Asante delineates an Afrocentric relationship for men and women. Williams judiciously points out how this relationship is sexist and grounded in Western patriarchal norms. She concludes by encouraging African American women to denounce Afrocentrism as long as it remains misogynistic and sexist.

In her essay, "A Womanist Response to the Afrocentric Idea: Jarena Lee, Womanist Preacher," Lorine L. Cummings joins the other authors in highlighting the sexist nature of Asante's Afrocentric thought. She argues, in a fashion similar to Williams, that "the African American woman is minimally involved in the foundational precepts of the Afrocentric idea" and that, where they are involved, patriarchal ideology is perpetuated. In spite of Asante's particular version of Afrocentrism, however, Cummings argues that the womanist and Afrocentric visions have merged historically in African American women's lives. She illustrates this point by examining the life and experiences of Jarena Lee. Cummings shows, for instance, how Lee's "in-spite-of faith" was decidedly Afrocentric and womanist as it empowered Lee to reject the "definitions of ministry that were imposed on her by society and by the African American church." She concludes her essay by offering Jarena Lee's life as a paradigm for contemporary African American women preachers.

Part One concludes with Kelly Brown Douglas's "To Reflect the Image of God: A Womanist Perspective on Right Relationship" examines the relationships which enslaved women forged with their communities, each other, and their men. Referring to these relationships as "a womanist way of relating," Douglas argues that these relationships were the foundation of the community's survival and wholeness in face of the tyrannies of chattel slavery. Unlike the Afrocentric relationships

that Asante delineates, a womanist way of relating is characterized by "reciprocal relationships of mutuality, especially
with men." Douglas urges the African American church and
community to return to a womanist way of relating as it faces
its current crisis. She concludes by suggesting that a womanist
way of relating would not only nurture life and wholeness for
African American women and men but that it would also reflect what it means to be created in the image of God.

Part Two, "Interpretation," explores the implications of
womanist and Afrocentric thought for interpretation. In this
section, womanist scholars highlight aspects of the Bible and
African American women's literature as reflective of womanist
and Afrocentric concerns. In her essay, "Slavery as a Sacred
Text: Witnessing in *Dessa Rose*," Deborah E. McDowell brings
an implicit womanist hermeneutic to the work of Sherley
Anne Williams. McDowell begins by pointing out that many
African American female writers have deemed slavery a sacred
text, that is, these writers have struggled to find "their own
words in the sprawling discourse on slavery." McDowell illustrates this point in a thoughtful explication of Williams's *Dessa
Rose*. She concludes that this novel, as well as others on slavery,
"witnesses slavery after freedom in order to engrave that past
on the memory of the present, but more importantly, on
future generations" so as to circumvent a "cultural amnesia"
that threatens to re-enslave us all.

Youtha C. Hardman-Cromwell's "Living in the Intersection of Womanism and Afrocentrism: Black Women Writers"
argues that black female writers gave expression to womanism
and Afrocentrism long before the terms were coined by Alice
Walker and Molefi Asante. She contends that if a womanist is
one who claims and values her identity as African American
and female, and if an Afrocentrist views the world in light of
an identity with an African past, then "African American

women always have been living in the intersection of womanism and Afrocentrism and their writers have given expression
to this fact." Hardman-Cromwell then goes on to explore the
poetry of writers such as Zora Neale Hurston, Margaret
Walker, Maya Angelou, and Nikki Giovanni to support her
contention.

Cheryl J. Sanders's essay "Black Women in Biblical Perspective: Resistance, Affirmation, and Empowerment" begins
with a historical overview of ways in which African American
women have used the Bible from colonial times to the present.
She documents the importance of the Scriptures in the poetry
of Phillis Wheatley, in the political speeches of Maria Stewart,
in the thought of unlettered slave women, and in the autobiographies of four nineteenth-century black women preachers:
Zilpha Elaw, Julia Foote, Jarena Lee, and Amanda Berry
Smith. The Bible is also cited by black women educators and
activists of the twentieth century, including Mary McLeod Bethune, Nannie Helen Burroughs, and Marian Wright Edelman. Present efforts by contemporary African American
female preachers and biblical scholars to engage in the task of
biblical interpretation are briefly described. The major part of
the essay is then devoted to the discussion of the resistance
strategies, moral affirmations, and divine empowerment of African women in the Bible, with specific reference to Hagar,
Zipporah, the Queen of Sheba, and the Candace, Queen of the
Ethiopians.

Part Three, "Learning," looks at the implications of
womanist and Afrocentric thought for how we teach as theological educators. Kelly Brown Douglas in "Teaching Womanist Theology" reflects upon her experiences in teaching
womanist theology. She tells how her students helped her to
discover a method for teaching womanist theology that was
compatible with the womanist concept. She then goes on to
delineate a womanist pedagogy that includes: (1) dialogue

with African American women's history and with women engaged in the struggle for life and wholeness, (2) an encounter with the diversity of African American women's experiences, and (3) a critical analysis of that experience. Douglas concludes her essay by noting that the "most enduring lesson for womanist pedagogy is flexibility so as to embrace the complex and dynamic reality of black womanhood."

Cheryl Sanders's essay, "Afrocentric and Womanist Approaches to Theological Education," attempts to identify some of the key methodological and epistemological issues involved in the employment of Afrocentric and womanist pedagogies in theological education. The problem of the validation of knowledge, norms, and experience within the intersection of womanist and Afrocentric thought is a major concern of this essay. She cites the "ecumenical" Afrocentricity of Asante and the "exclusive" Afrocentricity of Yosef A. A. ben-Jochannan as two alternative approaches to the challenge of doing theological education in a predominantly black setting in harmony with the womanist concern to "equip the churches to love black people to wholeness."

Acknowledgments

◆◆◆◆◆◆◆◆◆◆◆◆◆◆◆◆◆◆◆◆◆◆◆◆◆◆◆◆◆◆◆

The authors and editor gratefully acknowledge the following for their permission to reprint these materials:

Chapter 5 is adapted from "Negotiating between Tenses: Witnessing Slavery after Freedom—*Dessa Rose*" from *Slavery and the Literary Imagination: Selected Papers from the English Institute*, ed. Deborah E. McDowell and Arnold Rampersand, copyright © 1987 The Johns Hopkins University Press; reprinted by permission. The excerpt from "Lady, Lady," is copyright © Anne Spencer; reprinted by permission of Chauncey E. Spencer. The poems "Gift" and "Lost My Voice? Of Course./for Beanie" from *Revolutionary Petunias and Other Poems* are copyright © 1972 Alice Walker; reprinted by permission of Harcourt Brace & Company and the Wendy Weil Agency. The excerpt from "For Us Who Dare Not Dare" from *Oh Pray My Wings Are Gonna Fit Me Well* is copyright © 1975 Maya Angelou; reprinted by permission of Random House, Inc. and Virago Press. The excerpts from "Rebirth" and "For Dark Women" from *For Dark Women and Others* by Satiafa (Vivian V. Gordon) are copyright © 1982 Lotus Press, Inc.; reprinted by permission. Excerpts from "Poem for Some Black Women," copyright © 1971 Carolyn Rodgers, and "I Have Been Hungry," copyright © 1968, 1969, 1970, 1971, 1972, 1973, 1975 Carolyn Rodgers from *how i got ovah: New and Selected Poems*; reprinted by permission of Doubleday, a division of Bantam Doubleday Dell Publishing Group, Inc. The excerpt from "no more love poems #1" from *for colored girls who have considered suicide when the rainbow is enuf* is copyright © 1975, 1976, 1977 Ntosake Shange; reprinted by permission of Simon and Schuster and Russell & Volkening. The excerpt from "Notes on Commercial Theater" from *Selected Poems of Langston Hughes* is copyright © 1948 Alfred A. Knopf; reprinted by permission of Alfred A. Knopf, a subsidary of Random House, Inc.

PART ◊ ONE
EXPERIENCE

1

We Have a Beautiful Mother

Womanist Musings on the Afrocentric Idea

◆◆◆◆◆◆◆◆◆◆◆◆◆◆◆◆◆◆◆◆◆◆◆◆◆◆◆◆◆◆◆◆◆

Cheryl Townsend Gilkes

*A*s a sociologist who specializes in African American life and culture, I pay particular attention to our religious experience, especially women's roles. But because of the work that I love to do, that I have chosen to do, that I feel led to do, I cannot avoid the implications of either the Afrocentric idea or the womanist idea. And when I focus on African American women, I am reminded of W. E. B. DuBois and Anna Julia Cooper, who observed that to attend to women or issues related to women involves focusing in on multiple realities in our community. Deborah King in fact uses the phrases "multiple jeopardy" and "multiple consciousness," to talk about the "complicatedness" of our reality—its multiple contingencies and the microscopic complexity.[1] So my reflections in some ways will necessarily be musings, something of a laundry list of ideas to try to integrate our thinking about both the Afrocentric idea and the womanist idea, particularly in the contemporary context. Our context dictates that we seek ways to liberate, to elevate, and to point the way of salvation to people who are African American and Christian. We are here because we believe we have a story to tell to the nation, and our experience has something special to say to the world.

Understanding from Within

The term *Afrocentric* is highly charged. When we first started using it, however, it was not loaded. It was just a way of saying where you stand when you are thinking and talking. As I was preparing these reflections I discovered my own mixed emotions about what has happened to the term and its meaning. Sometimes I cringe when I hear the term because it is used, abused, and misused. Sometimes we even use it in ways that open it up for bothersome and inaccurate proclamations from the other side.

My own work as a sociologist has been aimed at correcting and redirecting thinking about African Americans. I came into social science at a time when sociology professors stood up in class and lectured at me about my broken families and my tangle of pathology and the matriarchy that governed my life. I remember sitting and thinking, "What are they talking about?" So I raised my hand in class one day and said to the professor, "Are you sure this is true about black families? Which black families are you talking about?" Of course, I was thinking of my family—my parents have been married for more than fifty years, and all of my grandmothers as well as my great aunt lived with us at some point in my life. I used to bother my little friends because I told them I had three grandmothers, since my granddad was divorced and remarried. And what my mother's family liked about my father was that he treated his mother-in-law as well as he treated his own mother. Where do you read about black men like that? Since there were also some families in my church like that, I kept wondering, "Who is this woman talking about?" I knew my grandmother and my grandfather had not stayed together, but my mother and father were doing a perfectly good job of it. And in crises or occasionally if they had a really bad argument, they would get down on their knees and pray together, and I would say, "Hmmm, I guess we don't have to worry, they're still here. They're going to be together for a while." There was always that kind of security at home. So when people started talking about the trouble in my black family, I raised my hand and said, "Who are you talking about?" And the professor said, "Well, the Moynihan Report said this." I said, "Yes." And she said, "He was quoting a black sociologist named E. Franklin Frazier."[2] So I went and read the book. I found out that Patrick Moynihan may have quoted Frazier, but he was highly selective in what he quoted. Many chapters he did not quote, and, where he did, he miscast words that Frazier had used, reworking them in a way I do not think Frazier had intended. I went back to her and I said, "You know there are a lot of other chapters in the book, and Frazier was not saying that mother-headed households were essentially pathological and that father-headed households were essentially always organized."

I also saw the damage that could be done when people are turned loose in social-work practicums in black housing projects with presumptions about black people that do real damage to people's lives. And I said, "There's something wrong here. Why is it that I have a different view of black women than all these other people do?" I grew up with black women as my role models. Where did they come from?

Then I remembered there was this thing at church called Women's Day. Yes, we sisters in the ministry know that it is tokenism; we know that. But there is another side to it. (This is why we as a people always have to think in terms of "both-and," not "either-or." We cannot think in binary oppositions because then we miss pieces of reality.) It wasn't Easter and it wasn't Christmas, but you knew it was a special day, because it was a day your mother jammed your hat on your head, dragged you out of the house early, and you didn't have to say a piece. And people always listened, and talked to the woman speaker afterwards. It made such an impression, as I realized later on when I met Pearl Olivia Stokes. She had spoken at my church when I was about seven or eight years old. I was able to speak to her in the early 1980s, describe back to her the suit she had worn, and hear her say, "Yes, you remember." So those kinds of "token" events do make a difference; they create a different worldview. So when Betty Friedan was saying that there is this "problem with no name" and that growing up she never knew any woman of substance, and that was the problem for American women—that was not my problem! I had to stand squarely in my tradition and realize that nobody knew the joys and encouragements that I had seen. The black women role models in my life indicated to me that the sociology of the black community needs to be done from within.

I also noticed that certain issues would always come up, and I realized that some of these differences in black people's lives made a positive but unnoticed difference. For instance, a paper that I wrote on "The Black Church as a Therapeutic Community" came about because I went to a lecture by R. D. Laing. He had a theory that people's craziness is intelligible. Laing thought that if you can spend time learning about the context of a person's life and see what is going on around her or him, that person's craziness makes sense. It is not good for them, but you can figure out the sources of it. That is a time-consuming approach—doing psychiatry like a "tarrying" service—and we don't have time for it in this culture. In any case, at this lecture people were getting up and talking about many alternative therapies. Listening, I said, "Hmmm, one of them sounded like things that went on in my church: shouting. People are going out and paying fifty to a hundred dollars to learn how to do this? An hour?" Then I discovered an anomaly in the statistics in the 1950s. If we take white people as the norm, we can posit that when there is a certain degree of poverty, there will be a certain amount or incidence of mental illness. We have the poverty—we have more than enough poverty—but not quite so much craziness as we should have, being poor. Why? Because differences that make a positive difference are ignored. Our negative differences are banner headlines. But whatever measurable survival skills we have, whatever strategies for life and survival that may make a positive difference, end up in footnotes in Urban League publications, not in publications widely read by those who make policy and decide what laws should apply to families, households, communities. My conviction grew that somebody had to be doing sociology from within the black community. A sociology that said what black people said and thought about themselves should be the starting point and framework for our questions. Still, we were not using the word *Afrocentric* at this point.

Then in my own encounter with my faith and my calling, something happened in the context of a research project I initiated on the sanctified church. The research project really started because someone in my community who was familiar with the sociology I had done on black women said, "Gee, we need to study the sanctified church." And of course the "sanctified church" was not in anybody's index. And I remember saying I am going to do this research using the term that black people use for themselves. Because you know how it is; you ask somebody, "What church are you with?" And they say, "I'm in a sanctified church." And you say, "Oh, okay." And they know that you know about the sanctified church, but you don't know enough about it to say which one. But if you say, "Which one?" then people know that you know enough about their experience to locate them in a very complex map of the African American religious experience. Then you could go on and talk because you are connected in certain ways. Knowledge is connection, and it extends the conversation. Some of the best friends I have came about because I knew to say, "Which one?" when they said they were in the sanctified church. So I was going to start with this term that black people have for their lives. And my method was going to grow out of black folks' definition of the situation. But when I went to do the literature review, there was nothing in the indexes about "sanctified church." I wanted to be culturally pure and to do this project from within the community, but not finding any literature was exasperating! Finally the librarian at Howard University School of Divinity took pity on me, and she whispered, "Look under sects and cults." Now I said, "Thank you" to her outwardly, but inwardly I thought "Arghhh! She's calling them deviant religions. They're not sects and cults. They are churches." Sociologists know the differences. Sects and cults are the deviant ones, and the church is the norm, according to the way in which European sociology of religion frames things. So this was a further step along the way, although we were still not using the term *Afrocentric* at that point.

Afrocentric Antecedents

Evenutally, however, a few people did start to use the term *Afrocentric*. It signifies a commitment to standing in the middle of the black experience, either in the United States or in Africa or worldwide, and starting one's thinking there. That is hard to do, in part because people do not understand your language. You say "sanctified church." They say, "What's that?" You say "Women's Day." They say, "What's that?" And the truth is that if we don't understand something, we assume there must be something wrong with it.

And so Afrocentricity becomes, as we name it now, part of a large ideal and strategy which is actually old in our community. I think one can say the Afrocentric idea existed among those slaves who told missionaries and others who wanted to know about black folks, to talk to the folks who have lived it. The Afrocentric idea starts with folks like W. E. B. DuBois (1868–1963), who tried to center his analysis in the African American experience and who in the process produced the first community study ever in the history of sociology in the United States.[3] If any of you have ever taken a college course in introductory sociology (unless you took it at a black college), did you learn that? There is one sociology textbook now that talks about the importance of DuBois, but it is authored by a white conservative who thinks soul is wonderful!

DuBois centered his analysis in the black community, and he did it with such integrity that when Max Weber was putting together a yearbook on sociologists in various nations he picked DuBois as the representative for the United States to talk about the black question. So DuBois represented us centrally; when we reread him, his nineteenth-century thinking sometimes stumbles a little, but DuBois was there. One can say his thinking, his message, his squaring himself within the African American experience is what we would call Afrocentric.

We might also mention Carter G. Woodson (1875–1950), who thought so much of the importance of our experience and believed that speaking to ignorance would make a difference. Woodson not only did the history and scholarship, he also organized the Association for the Study of Negro Life and History (now Afro-American Life and History) in Washington, D.C., and gave us what was then Negro History Week and is now Black History Month or African American History Month. He did so at a time when we were segregated, when the vast majority of black people were still in the South, where, we sometimes need reminding, a majority of black people still live. But Woodson organized it so that teachers who were limited in what they had to share could utilize the space that they had within the indirect-rule colonial structures where they worked to teach us about ourselves. It was only when we moved North, or got integrated, that we realized that those who were committed to teaching us a little bit about who we are and fostering our sense of ourselves as poets, as leaders, as thinkers, as talented, giving people, had all of a sudden disappeared from school life. We have been struggling to recover it. I think that Woodson's strategy helped in our struggle to recover what we realize we lost, in the context of what I call the dialectics of segregation. That dialectic included oppression, exclusion, and the lack of resources, on the one hand, and having teachers who loved us and were committed to us, on the other. He worked through that duality with someone like Nannie Helen Burroughs, who in constructing a training school for industrial education insisted that the graduation requirement include orations on Afro-American history.

So I believe we have to call these people Afrocentric in their thinking, if we take seriously Afrocentric thinking as an ideal and as a strategy for our community. Anna Julia Cooper, for instance, believed black people had much to share and to tell the nation. She felt that the diversity of black people had to be considered and that part of the racism of this society was its presumption of certain uniformities that were not true. She also insisted that the status of black women was essentially a measure of the status of the society. Gauging the state of the society by the situation of black people is a way of being Afrocentric as well. And even Booker T. Washington! As much trouble as we give Booker T. Washington, still *Afro-American* is a term associated with the Washington side of the movement. Margaret Murray Washington was the head of the National Federation of Afro-American Women.

Finally, we use the term *Afrocentric* now, but maybe we need, as Asa Hilliard has suggested, to remind ourselves to get the words straight. We say Afro-centric, but there is no Afro-ca. It's Africa, and Africentric. We borrowed *Afro* as a counter to *Euro*, and it has become the convention to say Afrocentric. Occasionally I have written *Africentric* and then gone to the mat with editors on it. We've got this wonderful word, which itself might be a wee bit flawed, but it helps a little.

Scholars have been struggling with the issues of African identity for a long time. Even during slavery, black leaders were talking about a historic past that remained important, that should not be denigrated, and that could stand with the other cultural legacies in the world. A neglected but helpful volume is Thomas F. Gossett's *Race: The History of an Idea in America*.[4] We do not realize just how recent the invention of race is. I am almost tempted to replace the word *race* with the phrase "Continent of origin in 1492." What was your continent of origin in 1492? At the root of race is the politics of how you came to be involved in the modern world system. Gossett's book details how scholars constructed whole disciplines around proving that black people are inferior and, ironically, how some of the white anti-racists make the important observation that race is not biological. It is social and political. They saw clearly, too, that the reason whites feel supreme is because they get praised, while black people are made inferior because they are not praised. In other words, the inspirational dimension of the politics of knowledge was recognized by both blacks and whites as an aspect of the process by which race and racism were being constructed and used against us.

We also have the work of G. G. James's *Stolen Legacy*, which reminds us that someone had talked about the Egyptian roots of Greek thinking quite some time ago.[5] We also had J. A. Rogers, who was constantly pruning the popular consciousness through his work. Not just his books, but also his newspaper articles in places like the *Pittsburgh Courier* let ordinary folk know who they were. He also coined the phrase "the world's greatest men of color." Old issues such as these have been carried forward in the newer conversation, and I will return to some of them.

Explicit concern for Afrocentricity begins when Molefi Kete Asante, in his books *Afrocentricity* and *The Afrocentric Idea*, invited us to think in alternative ways, to look into historic African cultures and think of the alternatives.[6] But Asante built to some extent on the work of Cheikh A. Diop, especially Diop's *The African Origin of Civilization*.[7]

Afrocentrism, Inspirational History, and Public Education

I became concerned as I started to read newspaper accounts of the Afrocentric movement and of academic departments and theorists that would bypass our older scholars like DuBois and Woodson to create a countertheory to the perceived theories of Europe. I sometimes wonder, are we refashioning the master's tools, by making a set of rigid theories, a "school of thought," to go out and test?

The Afrocentric idea has also become a source of misguided and racist public controversy. In the popular press advocates of Afroncentrism have been accused of being historical separatists and reverse racists and of writing inspirational history. But the problem with the latter charge is its presumption that professional historians, properly trained, do not write inspirational history. Yet, in major research libraries, what are the sources for doing American history? They are the gathered family papers of prominent people who were deemed heroes and invited to contribute their papers to those collections so historians would have something to work with.

Inspirational history stands behind the distortions we learned in grammar school. Every holiday had some curriculum unit, in which we learned a particular perspective on that historic event. In my eighth-grade class, wearing my mother's old wedding dress, I played a Bach minuet while the class did a minuet to celebrate George Washington's birthday in a play. I was "dressed to the nines" in a satin dress, and I felt so very revolutionary! No one ever said a word about him as a slaveowner. Nor did anyone ever talk about Thomas Jefferson as a slaveowner. Even today, when I sit in lectures and hear political scientists rhapsodize about the great ideas of Thomas Jefferson, President of the United States, I add, "and slaveowner." And they say, "Oh yes, yes, and slaveowner." People in Europe are shocked to learn that the fathers of democracy owned slaves. Yet we took it for granted. I am always telling my white students how I learned the inspirational history of the dominant culture. Afrocentrists have been accused of writing inspirational history, but in many instances they are merely correcting and adding pertinent details to the history that has already been presented to us.

We are also part of a crisis in public education that we have to recognize that we started and we do need to follow through. In the 1960s some black parents did recognize that there was something wrong with what was being taught, as did others later. Jewish parents, for instance, also discovered that their experience was missing from the curricula in communities where they lived. Nathan Glazer has shown how the Black Power movement provided other ethnic groups in the society with a vocabulary for articulating their concerns, asserting their identity, and moving against their own invisibility.[8] The movement was, to borrow DuBois's phrase, the gift of black folk.

The crisis in public education regards whose story will be told. And what does it mean when black and white children sit and look across a table at one another and one side wonders, "Your ancestors were slaves?" And the other side wonders, "Your ancestors beat my ancestors?" We don't want to be confronted by truths of the moral choices made by our historic community. So the politics of public education includes defenses of a particular view of the world that reflects the dominance of that group.

Such issues figure mightily in devising strategies for multicultural education. The assault on multiculturalism, led by people like Allan Bloom and Arthur Schlesinger, is part of the attempt to maintain white supremacy in our society.[9] We have to be clear about that. Afrocentrism can be an element as we devise strategies for multicultural education, but we need to be sure, as we use the term *Afrocentric*, that in the necessary politics and strategies we not put ourselves into ideological straightjackets that we may ourselves not fully understand and control. That's another musing.

Race, Color, and Cultural Presumptions

So Afrocentrism is an important public challenge to white supremacist myths and the intellectual mystifications that come out of fields such as history, political science, and my field, sociology. It is a challenge to certain kinds of presumptuousness. James Baldwin once wrote a wonderful short article for *Essence* about "On Being White and Other Lies."[10] He didn't use the term *myths*, he used the term *lies*. We too have to be careful that when we use the Afrocentric concept we do not read the race of Americans back into antiquity. Part of why Frank Snowden is having problems making his voice heard, in his studies of how blacks were viewed in antiquity, is that his works do not simply take the American definition and drive it backward into a time when "race" as such did not exist.[11]

We live the paradox of challenging whites on the basis of their definition of race, a task our ancestors understood clearly. When the slave preacher said, "God's gonna separate the sheep from the goats, and we know who has the wool," people got the point. It's the same challenge today. When I was teaching my African American Religious Experience class, and we were reading Robert Hood's book *Must God Remain Greek?*[12] I was trying to get them to understand the images of race and color that they had been living with and what the biblical images were. In one class we discussed Rev. 1:14, where the Son of Man is described as having hair of white wool. I hadn't had a haircut for a while, and I asked, "Who in this room has hair like lamb's wool?" They started to sweat because for them to admit that their professor, the only black person in the room, had hair like lamb's wool meant that the images of Jesus they had lived with all their lives might pose a problem. So they fidgeted and looked around the room until they finally lighted on this one student who had dark brown curly hair. (You have to understand, Colby College is not just a predominantly white liberal arts college—it is a *very* white one. Some of the white professors complain about the lack of diversity for white people, and I do have a lot of blonde-haired, blue-eyed students up in northern New England!) And he got nervous, because his racial status was coming into question. All of a sudden, the racial ambiguity, the phenotypic ambiguity that he had been carrying around was coming into crisis, and so he looked at me and said, "Her!" It was as if he had said, "*I* don't have hair like lamb's wool!" I was glad because I wanted them to struggle with that, with the iconography that runs deep into our psyche. The public Afrocentric challenge to white presumptuousness (namely, the modern American construction) does employ a relatively recent and unique definition of race, and say, "All right, if race means simply African ancestry, and not appearance, then let's take seriously *all* the African ancestry and let's take the *whole* continent, not just part of the continent. Let's see who really is of color in this world." So, ironically, Afrocentrists are working with a definition of race that allowed American slavers to define into one "race" diverse peoples from all over Africa so that the available pool for their slave labor force was as broad as possible. In a further irony, descendants of those many peoples have now in fact become as they were defined—one people.

The Afrocentric concept also challenges the white supremacist myth by breaking down the layers of racism, United-States-style. That is, racism is seen to be not just the economic exploitation, not just the political subordination and exclusion, but also the systematic cultural humiliation that Woodson identified in America's great miseducation. Afrocentrism identifies the cultural humiliation tied to this thing called racism. The cultural component is never not there, even in the foundations of higher education. That is why I always call the Western Civilization requirement White Supremacy 101. I don't know how many of you went to college where Western Civ was absolutely required for graduation. I was lucky that, in lieu of Western Civilization, I got to take some courses in Russian, Ancient Rome, African art, Southeast Asia—I had a ball! I also had a job working with a white student at the Berkeley School of Music, where students major in things like jazz. (Some of these children want to be jazz musicians, but their parents want them to have a bachelor's degree!) He was worried about graduation. When I asked why, he said, "I can't pass Western Civ, and we have to have Western Civ to graduate from Berkeley School of Music." I was wondering, "What in the world does Western Civ have to do with jazz?" I said to him, "Why are you having trouble passing Western Civ?" Now if you know anything about jazz, you know that to become a jazz musician you do not take classes. You go and take your instrument and sit with the people you want to learn under, until they invite you to play—usually until one or two o'clock in the morning. So when Western Civ called at eight o'clock, he couldn't get out of bed! That's why he had been trying to pass Western Civ for years. I said, "Does the college have a course in black history?" He said, "No." Western Civ was required, but there was no African-culture or black-history requirement nor a course in it. Yet students were majoring in the music that was rooted in the African experience in the United States. Cultural humiliation has to do with the power to define what is important in institutions and then enforcing it, like terrifying this young white man about not getting his degree while he's trying to become a jazz musician. Part of the task is challenging the content and ownership of this Western canon, a particularly pernicious form of cultural dominance. As Henry Louis Gates asks, whose canon is it, anyway?[13]

Afrocentering

Juxtaposing the Afrocentric idea and the womanist idea points to two interrelated tasks. One is centering the black experience in the human experience, which is part of our task of fighting racism and asserting our humanity in a society that says we are somewhat less than human. A way that we do that in the academy is to learn about the human experience through the liberal arts. But our second task is centering the human experience from the point of view of the black experience. It is an exercise for the head, but also for the heart. We have to believe in it. It grows out of our unshakable belief in the importance of telling the story over and over again, not just in an academic, formal way, but also telling our children. That is where we intersect with the womanist idea. What's in that idea for us?

My assumption is that Alice Walker's definition of womanist is decidedly Afrocentric, although not all thinking about Afrocentrism is womanist. Hers is Afrocentric because, first of all, she builds. She digs right into the core of the historical black experience to pull together this definition in *In Search of Our Mothers' Gardens.*[14] As in a dictionary definition, she argues that a womanist is a black feminist, an idea involving such qualities as being challenging and bold, being inquiring, pushing and straining toward a special kind of maturity. The idea involves love, being relational, being committed to health and survival, which she says so well in the title of an essay called "Breaking Chains and Encouraging Life."

Second, to be a good womanist, one must be universalist toward ourselves as a people, loving all of ourselves. If one asks, "Mama, why are our cousins one set of colors, and why are we another set of colors?" Walker would respond, "The colored race is like a flower garden, it includes all." Despite the way in which the boundaries have been built around us, we are the most genetically diverse population in the United States, probably in the world. And so womanist is universalist, grounded in strength and the presumption of capability. It's good for ourselves.

Third, Walker's definition is culturally coded. Its elements reflect African women's historical, cultural, and spiritual experience, especially when it talks about "loves food, loves roundness, loves the moon, loves dance, loves the Spirit, loves herself, regardless" of how much the culture tries to communicate to her that she is ugly, that she should get back, that she should maybe not stick around, all those old notions. In spite of such cultural assaults, there is determination and perhaps support within community for self-love, enabling us to be and feel relational, committed, capable, inquiring. The womanist idea, in Alice Walker's thinking, is an Afrocentric vision, indeed one influenced by Howard Thurman and Martin Luther King, Jr.

Womanism Retelling the Story

To see the artistic vision underlying these ideas, it is important that we explore Alice Walker's chief Afrocentric text, *The Temple of My Familiar*.[15] When this novel appeared, after *The Color Purple*, reviewers jumped on it with both feet. They had no idea what Alice Walker was doing in the book, with its character who has lived many lives, its telling many different kinds of stories, and its moving back and forth between Central America and Latin America and the United States and Africa. Only when one thinks of womanist as Afrocentric does it become clear what Walker was doing in this text. She has taken some of her womanist ideas and tried to run them through narratively. She has taken into account the debate about human beings and tried to resolve it in a way that rejected racism but pushed for a larger, relational, humanist vision. And she has recovered some classical myths, reread them, and asked, Where was our mother, our black mother Africa in all of this?

It is an almost constant question. For instance, she takes the old myth of the Gorgon's head—the three snake-haired sisters in Greek mythology whose appearance turns people to stone and whom Perseus beheads without gazing at them. Walker rereads that ancient myth as part of the story of the destruction of black civilization. She looks seriously at the Gorgon's head and sees not a monster woman with snakes for hair but a black woman with dreadlocks. Or she looks at the lion of Judah, the ancient symbol of one of the Israelite tribes, and sees dreadlocks in its mane. Part of what her text is saying is that the African woman as mother of civilization keeps asserting herself in all these stories and pieces of memory. Walker takes seriously the myth of Eden, too, and tries to read back beyond it to ask, What happened before Eden fell? What made people cover themselves, run away, and become hostile? She attempts to explain existence before the Fall and what happens when people begin to kill animals (you know her stand on animal rights). When human beings start to be violent to others in their environment, how long will it be before they become violent toward each other on the basis of distinctions and gradations? Walker also takes seriously the myths that black people have, the folklore of black people. We have so many stories about what it was like when God still walked around on the earth and talked to the animals. And native Americans have the same things, too. Walker is trying to reconcile some of the parallels in this book through the character's telling stories out of her life. Historically, she contextualizes the transformation of Europe, showing how the reconquest of Spain from the Muslims coincided with the emergence of anti-Africanism.

Walker's novel is also a cautionary tale. She goes back and tries to detail what happened on the African continent to us. How did we get into conflicts as African people that led to our enslavement? We must beware of people who say, "Oh, they were enslaving their own people," because people don't enslave their own people. No, these were different African groups and nations in conflict with one another. What was the nature of their conflicts? And how was traditional African culture, with its affirmation of women and their role, suppressed during the conquest of Africa? She asks all these questions in this ambitious and amazing book. No wonder the reviewers went crazy! *The Temple of My Familiar* is, then, a critique and a vision. It raises up what we as human beings in the contemporary era have to work through in order to restore a compassionate humanism that totally eschews racism and brings us across barriers even of class. Walker is struggling with all of that in that text, and she offers a strategy for asking questions without going overboard in one way or another. As she constantly discovers and recovers myths, she asks how can we explain the destruction, explain the hostility toward women of African descent, and what must we do as human beings to come together again?

Womanism and Human Solidarity

When I worked for the Black Women's Oral History Project, I had the privilege of interviewing Queen Mother Moore. It was an experience. She was a witty, wonderful woman whose entire life unfolded like a jewel of single-minded commitment to the liberation and advancement of black people. She described the importance of Marcus Garvey in her life, particularly his seeing Africa as a center of the world and his lighting a passionate fire within her that made Africa central to her definition of herself. And Africa became central to her sense of mission to and in America. She talked to me about going to old bookstores and finding old maps where the Atlantic Ocean was referred to as the Ethiopian Ocean or Sea. The Atlantic world was the Ethiopian world.

Queen Mother Moore talked about all these little discoveries and about the kind of life that she had led. She described her experience growing up in a Louisiana family where her father was a very, very light Louisiana Creole who married a brown-skinned woman. She said, "My mother was your color." She was trying to get me to understand the context of the family. She said, "My father's family stopped speaking to him when he married her. That's the kind of problem we have as a people." Then she talked about the luxury she was raised in. She said, "When I was going to school, when I was five years old, my nurse was taking me to school, and as I was going to school I discovered I had a hole in my handkerchief. I ordered my nurse to go back and get me another handkerchief." And then she leaned across the desk, and she looked at me and said, "Honey, I was raised to be a real bourgeois stinker." That was her self-description.

She also talked about going from the bourgeois stinker part of her life to the discovery of what she called black people's oppressive psychoneurosis. That was her word for it. Somehow we had lost our right mind, our African mind. And in the process of losing our African mind, we were cooperating too handily with our oppression in America. When I interviewed her in 1977, she was in her early eighties, and she was an abbess for the Ethiopian Orthodox Church of North America in Brooklyn. She and I had a good time, but during the time of the interview, she looked at me and got very serious and said, "Honey, I don't want equality." Inside I'm saying, "What is she going to say?" And then she took a deep breath, and she said, "I want supremacy!" And when she said that, I realized the poverty of my own liberalism. It just sort of passed before my eyes as I waited for her to continue.

What did she mean? She was a nationalist who was no longer really a separatist but who believed that what black people had suffered in this land gave them a right to define their own culture and politics and economics. She said no group, not even the Communist Party (and she had belonged to the Communist Party as well, and was grateful to the party because it had given her an analysis of political economy and a way of looking at history), understood what needed to be done for black people in America. She gave me an example, the struggle to integrate baseball. She said, "I regret that now. We struggled to get black players into the white leagues, but we should have struggled to get the black teams into the leagues, because we lost our managers and our owners."

Having interviewed many elders, I learned how their thinking had changed. Our understanding of ourselves changed because these elders, who had tried and discovered and learned, told the story to someone else to change the strategy. But she was convinced that no one could speak for black people but black people. And black people were not going to solve their problems until they shook off oppression. In a society characterized by the kind of racism we had known, I talked about this peculiar but historically specific combination of cultural humiliation, economic exploitation, and political exclusion and subordination. You've got to take that all as one big knot; they all work together for evil purposes in this society. She felt the only possible healing could come through power.

Queen Mother Moore's vision is womanist insofar as it makes the connections with the larger project of human solidarity. That is where the Afrocentric idea and the womanist idea connect. The womanist idea is utopian, and it cannot be fulfilled under threat and constant defensiveness. It is not separatist, Alice Walker says, except periodically, for health and healing.

Patricia Hill Collins argues that the recurring humanist vision is central to black feminism. When she says humanist, she does not mean antireligious. She means a vision or ideal of humanity, mercy, compassion, human solidarity. Collins writes, "Without a commitment to human solidarity . . . any political movement—whether nationalist, feminist or anti-elitist—may be doomed to ultimate failure."[16] The words and actions of black women intellectuals from different historical times and addressing markedly different audiences resonate with a strikingly similar theme of the oneness of all human life. And in the process Collins reminds us how important it is to connect with the voices of the past. Yes, we have a new idea, but we must not cut ourselves off from the past by pursuing that idea without rooting it and grounding it in its antecedents. No one person can own it.

"Perhaps the most succinct version of the humanist vision in black feminist thought," says Collins, "is offered by Fannie Lou Hamer, the daughter of sharecroppers and a Mississippi civil rights activist. 'Ain' no such thing as I can hate anybody and hope to see God's face.' "[17] Taken together, the ideas of Anna Julia Cooper, Pauli Murray, Alice Walker, and other black women intellectuals too numerous to mention, suggest a powerful answer to the question, What is black feminism, or what is womanism? Inherent in their words and deeds is a definition of black feminism as a process of self-conscious struggle that empowers women and men to actualize a humanist—that is, a humane, universalist, and compassionate— vision of the community.

Perhaps the deepest and most dramatic issue in the Afrocentrist discussion is the struggle over images of God and God's people. It is a struggle over the anthropology and origins of what we now call world religions, especially those now considered to be the Abrahamic religions, Judaism, Christianity, and Islam. The womanist response actually is not a response but a position, one that roots God in the Spirit who is loved. The womanist position is that we cannot know, but we can love and strive boldly. Ultimately we will adopt Afrocentrist ideas and strategies insofar as they heal us, take us back to old landmarks, empower us to lead and guide others to liberation, and help us to build a compassionate world. Only those kinds of Afrocentric ideas are also womanist.

2

Afrocentrism and Male-Female Relations in Church and Society

◆◆◆◆◆◆◆◆◆◆◆◆◆◆◆◆◆◆◆◆◆◆◆◆◆◆◆◆◆◆◆◆◆◆◆

Delores S. Williams

*I*n this chapter I have set four tasks for myself. After voicing my reservations as well as proclivities for the subject, I will give a critical description of Afrocentricism. Then I will discuss male and female relationships in the context of the Afrocentric notion of how these relationships ought to be constituted. Finally I will indicate what I see to be the limitations of Afrocentrism with regard to women's relations to men and with regard to the black church. My insights about Afrocentrism are informed by the work of Molefi Kete Asante—especially his book entitled *Afrocentricity*.

Afrocentrisms Old and New

At the outset I must confess. I have reservations about the subject, i.e., Afrocentrism and male-female relations in church and society. On the one hand, my intellectual intuition and my "school-of-hard-knocks" education in grassroots Kentucky tell me that it is too late in the day of black people's lives in America to consider this topic. I think we black people traveled a route to Afrocentrism in the 1960s and 1970s. Cultural nationalists like Amiri Imamu Baraka and Ron Karenga urged us to take African names for ourselves—as do the Afrocentric proponents today. People like Baraka and Karenga urged us to put African heritage and Afro-American culture and history at the center of our lives and consciousness—as do Afrocentric proponents today. We donned our dashikis, our new African names, our Afros; we read black authors and did black rituals screaming over and over: "Down with whitey's culture and history and up with Afro-American culture and history!" Now here we are in the 1990s playing a variation of the same tune and calling it "Afrocentrism," saying once again: "Down with white Western culture as the center of our consciousness and lives and up with African American history and culture and African heritage." It reminds me of a song we used to sing when I was a teenager entitled, "Here We Go 'Round in Circles," again and again and again.

Today, I wonder if this focus upon Afrocentrism and male-female relations in church and society is not a diversionary tactic—on the part of mainline American political forces—to keep us black people from asking the real question. And that question is this: What will be the terms for black people's economic, spiritual, educational, and physical survival in the "new world order" that George Bush and his cohorts announced? I am not optimistic about the fate of African Americans in this new ordering. With more than two million people homeless (and most of them black); with 27 percent of the AIDS cases in America being black (when we make up only 12 percent of the population); with almost 80 percent of our young people unemployed; with a high-school drop-out rate and a death rate among young black people unprecedented in our history; with drugs ravishing our communities, I ask myself: When we black people spend time on subjects like Afrocentrism and male-female relations, are we "out to lunch" while our black children and homeless black people suffer intellectual and physical death as well as spiritual starvation? Are we "out to lunch" while the powers that be are perhaps planning and executing the genocide of most black people, male and female?

On the other hand, I feel the relevance of our topic when I read Kariamu Welsh's description of Afrocentricity in Asante's book *Afrocentricity*. She says, "Afrocentricity resembles the black man, speaks to him, looks like him, and wants for him what he wants for himself."[1] Then she goes on practically to deify Asante as she likens him to the *male* luminaries in African American history: David Walker, Nat Turner, Marcus Garvey, Elijah Muhammad, Frederick Douglass, W. E. B. DuBois, Edward Blyden, Malcolm X, Karenga, Madhubuti, and Baraka. In her Foreword, Welsh does not mention a single woman. She does not say that Afrocentricity resembles black women. She does not say Afrocentricity looks like black women and wants for black women what they want for themselves. Black women's names and deeds are excluded from Welsh's words and from practically every page in the book— except those pages where Asante himself mentions the names of a few African goddesses and the name "Harriet," perhaps referring to Harriet Tubman. In what appears to be total contradiction, Welsh finally claims everyone is included in Afrocentricity.

There is no doubt in my mind that Asante's form of Afrocentricity in the book by that name is woman-exclusive while it pretends to be inclusive of all black people. In his chapter entitled "The Essential Grounds," he lifts up from African

American history the figures important for an understanding of what Afrocentrism is. The figures are all male: Booker T. Washington, Marcus Garvey, Martin Luther King, Jr., Elijah Muhammad, W. E. B. DuBois, Malcolm X, and Karenga. Rosa Parks is referred to very briefly as Asante hastily moves on to credit King with developing the nonviolent movement in the United States in the 1960s.

Elements of Afrocentrism

So what specifically is this Afrocentricism besides woman-exclusive? According to its main proponent, Asante, Afrocentrism is a spiritual and philosophical ideology (a way of living, thinking, and knowing) that places African American history, culture and African heritage at the center of black people's lives. Afrocentrism involves black people's conversion from conditioned white consciousness to a new African American and African-centered thinking and acting. It involves the creation of ritual to support and reinforce new black consciousness. Afrocentrism affirms a universal African consciousness that is a collective consciousness. Describing this consciousness Asante says it:

> expresses our shared commitments, fraternal reactions to assaults on our humanity, collective awareness of our destiny, and respect for our ancestors. When we come to acceptance, as surely we are coming, of this consciousness we will experience the rise of Afrocentricity.[2]

Making allowances for the range of skin colors among African Americans, Asante says, "Afrocentricity . . . is only superficially related to color, it is more accurately a philosophical outlook determined by history."[3]

Through Afrocentric thinking and action African Americans become empowered and liberated, Asante suggests. This happens because they take over language and create it so that it speaks the truth about African American history and culture and about African heritage. In Asante's thought empowerment is associated with black nationalism. "What is necessary," he says, "is that the [black] national cause becomes the principal interest of the people and all other interests become subordinate considerations."[4] Three kinds of intelligence support the movement toward Afrocentricity and empowerment. These are creative intelligence, re-creative intelligence, and consumer intelligence. Creative intelligence designs new forms of consciousness and action. Re-creative intelligence expands these created designs and actions to new heights. Consumer intelligence makes use of and perpetuates what has been created and re-created. Consumer intelligence neither creates nor re-creates new forms. Of course, Asante points only to African American males as he illustrates this intelligence and nationalism. Black women are neither referred to nor singled out as examples in his discussion.

Women are invisible in Afrocentrism until Asante begins to define the nature of male-female relationships within Afrocentric thinking. As could be expected by those who know that the black community often associates the word *sacrifice* with black women's roles, Asante's Afrocentrism regards sacrifice as a vital component of male-female relations. So, in response to our subject of "Afrocentrism and Male-Female Relations in Church and Society," Asante's work says this: "There are four aspects to Afrocentric relationships: *sacrifice*, *inspiration*, *vision* and *victory*. In each of these aspects, we see elements of mutual respect and sharing." He is to be given credit here for attempting to improve black people's understanding by including black men in his notion of sacrifice in the relationship. He goes on to say:

> Sacrificial means that each partner is willing to give up certain aspects of himself or herself for the advancement of the people. Thus, the relationship is taken out of the individual context and placed into the collective context, becoming a part of the generative will of the people.[5]

But then he buys into white Western standards about womanhood and into old 1960s notions of black womanhood and black manhood when he says, "Every man should want his lady to be Isis, Harriet, Yaa Asantewaa and every woman should want a [Nat] Turner, Malcolm [X], Elijah Muhammad, King, Garvey."[6]

As used in the West, "lady" is a concept white patriarchy has created to signify the "pedestalization" of white womanhood and the devaluation of black womanhood. The black feminist essayist and thinker bell hooks has shown us this.[7] It is obvious (by his reference to African goddesses and extraordinary African and African American women) that Asante has taken up the notion of African American women as "superwomen"—a notion that black feminist writer Michele Wallace has shown to be devastating to black women's struggle to provide real and meaningful images of themselves.[8] Those of us who lived through the 1960s black cultural revolution know that it was the custom of many of the male revolutionaries to refer to black women in exalted terms like queen, earth mamma, and "queen of the Nile." In their rhetoric and poetry, few of the revolutionaries seemed interested in ordinary, hard-working black women. And black men were referred to as kings or black heroes who had accomplished significant feats for black people. When black men changed their given or "slave" names, they often took the names of African kings or heroes. Thus Asante resorts to this way of thinking when he expresses the hope of black men choosing

"superwomen" as partners and black women choosing "super-
men" like the male liberation figures of black history.
Individual freedom in male-female relationships is subordinate to the group's demands, according to Asante. He claims
all relationships are subject to "whatever is necessary for the
collective will of the people. . . . A woman's time to create and
a man's time to produce must be looked upon as a giving to
the collective will."[9] One of the problems for black women
here is that Asante's reference to women creating and men
producing sounds like some of the 1960s black nationalist pro-
paganda that claimed black women's roles were to reproduce
babies for the revolution. It was Stokely Carmichael who is ru-
mored to have said, in the heat of the 1960s cultural revolution,
that "a woman's position in the revolution is prone." I hope that
Afrocentric proponents, in their rush to craft an ideology consistent with black male needs, are not suggesting the same thing.
    Continuing to describe the appropriate character of male-
female relationships according to Afrocentric views, Asante says:

> Ultimately, the test of sacrifice is the willingness to be
> Afrocentric everywhere and at all costs. . . . The Afrocen-
> tric relation is also inspirational. You are stimulated by
> your interactions with your partner, not just physically,
> but emotionally, psychologically, and intellectually as
> well. . . . The man and woman in a relationship must be
> attuned to the primary objective of all Afrocentric
> unions: the productive and creative maintenance of the
> collective cognitive imperative. . . . [And the cognitive
> imperative] is the overwhelming power of a group of
> people thinking in the same direction . . . it is a full spiri-
> tual and intellectual commitment to a vision.[10]

Asante maintains that "relationships which are based upon
more than one . . . woman can also be based upon the princi-

ples of Afrocentricity." He claims that "while the couple is recognized as the most effective relationship in most cases, *Njia* [a Kiswahili word for 'the Way'] does not prescribe form but it does prescribe content." Further, "people must inspire each other toward correct and righteous Afrocentricity."[11]

In other words, a black man can have more than one woman or wife and still be Afrocentric. But no such provision is made for black women. Since he emphasizes content and not form, I suppose he means men can have relationships with any number of women as long as the entire entourage lives in accord with Afrocentric ideology and action. Hence victory in the relationships between men and women means that everything (love, thought, action, freedom) is subservient to the Afrocentric worldview presenting itself "clothed" with male examples.

A Womanist Critique

Several serious problems plague Asante's Afrocentric vision of male-female relationships. First, it is thoroughly sexist. He apparently adheres to white Western patriarchy's way of depicting women as either queens, goddesses, or temptresses. While he presents goddesses and superwomen for black men to prefer as mates, he provides an example of an improper male-female relationship in which blame falls on the black female who is portrayed as a temptress. Note this passage from Asante's *Afrocentricity*:

> In order to get the brother she wanted a sister went through numerous outer changes of sartorial fashions, hairstyles, and manner of speech. After he had begun relating to her she ceased her outer changes and the relationship went from bad to worse. She accused him of not

being interested in her for herself. . . . Indeed the sister
felt that the brother naturally responded to her display of
outward symbols of Afrocentricity. . . . However, the
brother, not being Afrocentric although aware of the
outer changes and possibilities, was seduced by superfi-
cialities.[12]

The "brother" is described as "seduced" rather than as having
exercised free choice in the matter. Thus the "brother" is re-
lieved of all responsibility while the "sister" bears the weight of
the problem because of her "seductiveness" and "shallowness."

In another place in the book where Asante, in his discussion of his coined word *afrology*,[13] is making the point that
professors do not have to be black to teach the Afrocentric
worldview, he once again assigns the negative burden of an
idea to women. Thus he writes:

However, many students did not see the fallacy of color
as a criterion for teaching afrology. . . . There are some
black professors who would, because of their total baptism in Western perspectives, argue that there exists no
particular black cultural data. Appointment of such black
professors to universities made little difference to the
conventional education process. . . . Students who de-
manded black professors quickly discovered that race did
not determine her sensitivity.[14]

The question here is why does the pronoun *her* get associated
with the problem the author describes? Nowhere else in this
section on afrology does the feminine pronoun appear. The
personal pronouns used are *he, we, they*. Let us hope that the
her in the quotation above is a misprint; at least that explana-
tion relieves the work from bordering on misogyny.

Second, there are problems with Asante's Afrocentric
vision of male-female relationships because—like his male pre-

decessors in the 1960s black cultural revolution—he romanti-
cizes African heritage. He gives no attention to the negative
aspects of that heritage, which African writers themselves portray in their works. For instance, Chinua Achebe's book
Things Fall Apart shows clearly how, in traditional African
society before colonialism, the strong (e.g., the character
Okonkwo the strong man) oppress and persecute the weak.[15]
Hence, whether the society is black or white, it seems
some things defy the color line to be what all societies pos-
sess in abundance: common human errors centered around
power.

Obviously Asante's Afrocentric lens has not focused upon
books by African women showing the oppression inherent in
traditional African social arrangements and practices before
colonialism. The African woman Buchi Emecheta has written
a book, *The Joys of Motherhood*, which reveals that traditional
African society was organized through polygamy so that
women's mothering, nurturing, and emotional capacities were
thoroughly exploited.[16] Awa Thiam, another African woman
writer, speaks out about the suffering inherent in traditional
African practices of clitoridectomy, infibulation and in
institutionalized polygamy. As a charge to African women, her
book is entitled *Black Sisters, Speak Out*.[17] Thus African
women tell of very old traditions and practices, dating back in
African heritage long before colonialism—traditions and practices that are still alive in many parts of Africa oppressing and
abusing African women.[18] Unless Asante and his cohorts
make a serious analysis of both positive and negative dimensions of African gender heritage, Afrocentrism's advocacy of
the dominance of the people's collective will can yield tyr-
anny that oppresses women as long as the Afrocentric vision
lives.

The third and gravest limitation of Asante's Afrocentrism is that its sexism and its support of male dominance make it a convenient instrument (along with white feminism) for helping to hold white male supremacy in place in the United States. An illustration can be given here. Because of its racist emphasis upon white women's experience and its way of ignoring racism as it achieves opportunities and advancement for white women, the white feminist movement has helped hold white supremacy in place in American society. By the same token, the Afrocentric movement—with its emphasis upon male experience and its way of ignoring the sexism shaping its vision—supports male supremacy in American society. Neither white feminists nor black Afrocentrics have sufficient power to block completely (and continuously) white male power to manipulate public opinion through media, money, and capital.

Thus white male power can manipulate white supremacy (supported by white feminism) and male dominance (supported by Afrocentrism) so that it serves the interest of white males and keeps most women and most blacks oppressed. What the proponents of Afrocentric vision ignore is that the fruits of an oppressed group's cultural transformation cannot be passed from generation to generation unless the group has the economic and military power (as well as power over educational systems) to sustain what it is trying to advance—especially if what it is trying to advance runs counter to the larger society's values, power structure, and sanctioned ways of thinking and acting. Without the power of manipulation on an expansive scale, an oppressed group's transformational yield will be obscured. And its negative "fallout" will be used to the advantage of the group having the most economic and military power to manipulate the society's communicative systems and institutions.

Black Christianity and
Afrocentric Sexism

More so than the advocates of Afrocentricity, the African American poet Margaret Walker has been realistic about what it will probably take for African Americans to obtain justice as well as economic and social equality in North America. In her poem "For My People," when she mentions the need for courageous black people to rise up and face down white oppression, she says these words: "Let a bloody peace be written in the sky."[19] Those of us who have lived long enough and have lived every day of our lives in white capitalist social, political, and economic structures believe that it will perhaps only be through bloodbaths that North American blacks achieve complete economic, cultural, political, and social justice for black people, female and male.

However, it is to Asante's credit that he sees the black church as having the numbers and resources to play a significant role in helping black people become more conscious of the character of African American history and African culture and heritage. He rightly sees hope in young black people coming back to the church transformed. His observations and question are significant when he says that they

> will make of the Black Church what the Ukrainians made of theirs, and what the Jews have made of their synagogues: places where children receive [black] cultural and historical training. Such training cannot be left to the schools. Since we have so many churches in the community with buildings going unused on Saturdays, why not Saturday schools?[20]

Asante is also right when he suggests that we need intellectual and spiritual resurrection in the African American community today. The black church can help greatly with this if it takes "Christianity . . . out of its white encasement and . . . [places] it in the ebony wrappings of the people's spirit as a transition to the total stripping to the bone of the church as it is presently constituted in order to be reclothed"[21] — reclothed in theology and action dedicated to the economic growth, to the positive and productive quality of life, and to the freedom of every black American, female and male. He correctly observes that African American history "shows that the church, sooner or later, establishes itself as the transmitter of the new visions within our community."[22]

Apparently Asante does not understand the degree to which Jesus Christ centers the theology of the black church and the lives of its members, especially the females. Thus he can simplistically state that "the church is only secondarily a theological institution, it is primarily a social institution concerned more with fellow-ship than with dogma."[23] He assumes here that dogma is a prerequisite for all theology and that if there is no formal doctrinal base the church has no theology. Though fellowship is important in the black church, its God-talk (theology) is just as important and has a lot to do with how the black church presents itself to the world and how it interprets its mission.

Asante wants the use of the church to spread his Afrocentric worldview, but he does not hanker after the religion to which the black church is presently committed. He believes:

> God must speak out on the subject of black liberation, and the churches must interpret God's answers for the church members. This interpretation must not be merely a repainting of Jesus to look black; it must be a theology which reflects our history. . . . The result of this change will be dramatic. Conversions to political theories and actions will break out on the religious horizon; ministers will preach doctrines based on new symbols. Black ma-

donnas will give way to new symbols arising out of the lives of [African goddesses and gods] Isis, Yaa Asantewaa, and Nzingha.[24]

Salvation will have to do with "Afrocentricity . . . [rising] on the sanctification and deification of our [black] history. . . ."[25] But salvation also has to do with liberation in Asante's thought. He believes the church will achieve this salvation on earth when it adopts the Afrocentric vision and consistently passes it along in the community.

However, if the church and the Afrocentric worldviews do not shed their sexism, they will remain little more than instruments that white male supremacy can use to oppress and control all black people. If Afrocentrism does not advocate addressing the terrible misogynist and sexist views some black church leaders have about the role, place, and person of black women in the church, then Afrocentrism will be of no value to black church women. If the proponents of Afrocentrism do not focus critical and judgmental eyes upon the mistreatment of women in traditional African heritage, they will only condone the suffering of African women today who experience traditional genital mutilation. If all the images, themes, and illustrations remain male in Afrocentric vision and writing, black women in the church would do future generations of black women a favor by refusing to allow Afrocentrism to spread in the church and society. Then sexist Afrocentrism—like its cousin, black nationalism of the 1960s—will only be a small, whimpering voice that never reaches maturity.

3

A Womanist Response to the Afrocentric Idea

Jarena Lee, Womanist Preacher

◆◆◆◆◆◆◆◆◆◆◆◆◆◆◆◆◆◆◆◆◆◆◆◆◆◆◆◆◆◆◆◆

Lorine L. Cummings

*W*omanism and Afrocentrism are compatible in that both use the African American experience as their point of departure and call for the utilization of African American role models and symbols. Conceptually, however, womanism and Afrocentrism differ. The womanist idea emerged because African American female voices had been left out of much of the traditional literature, whether theological or secular. No one sought to incorporate or include the struggles, experiences, and issues specifically related to African American women. Womanists articulate the voices of African American women with authenticity and authority. Eurocentric perspectives tended to be inclusive of both male and female as white feminists have articulated their experiences, while the African American woman's perspective has too often been subsumed into the African American male perspective. This process has resulted in a distorted and invalid representation of African American women.

No one can accurately reflect and/or speak about African American women better than ourselves. Others attempt to discuss their understanding of our experience, but they cannot tell the entire story. African American women have been telling their own story, but no one listened. Womanists are voicing concerns of African American women which are often very different from those articulated by their white female and African American male counterparts.

Womanism as Afrocentric

African American women have had to create a place for ourselves by raising our voices unapologetically in protest. Womanists embrace the definition outlined by Alice Walker in her book *In Search of Our Mothers' Gardens*.[1] This definition captures the essence of the character and strength of African American women who have often gone unnoticed, unheard, or simply ignored. Although some aspects of the definition are controversial, by and large those of us who could not fully accept feminism as necessarily relevant to our struggle discover that womanism expresses what heretofore has not been articulated. Womanism accurately reflects the African American woman's experience.

The fact that we had to distinguish ourselves and express a unique perspective is Afrocentrism in operation. Afrocentrists assert the African American's right to self-determination and the right to identify and name the parameters and character of our experience. Womanists and Afrocentrists rename, revisit, and reexamine traditionally held concepts and ideas about African Americans, affirming and validating this unique perspective. Our vision returns to our collective experience prior to slavery, and we embrace the totality of who we are both as Africans and as Americans. Our dual ancestry is accepted and we view ourselves before slavery; our roots remain African.[2]

The Afrocentrists present the African American male perspective, which too often defines African American women in traditional roles. African American men presume, without asking us, to know our voice and how we view the world. A unifying point of womanism and Afrocentrism is their focus on our heritage, legacy, and cultural richness. Yet Afrocentrists continue the patriarchal aspects of the Eurocentric male perspective, while womanists reflect on the entire African American community from a female perspective. While Afrocentrists assert the validity of a separate and distinct voice from the European one, womanists further that distinction by validating the unique perspective of African American women. While Afrocentrists link the experiences of African Americans with our African roots, calling for an integration of the Afrocentric perspective into the fabric of American culture, womanists assert that the African American woman's perspective must be included in Afrocentrism. Afrocentrists are not womanist, but womanists are Afrocentric. Womanists are concerned about the entire community and holistic in approach, which means that both men and women can come together in dialogue to define and address the needs of the entire African American community.

Afrocentrists lift up the concept of returning to one's true self, that is, asserting, reaffirming, and dedicating oneself to adopting African American role models to define who we are.[3] Womanists study the journals, diaries, and writings of African American women, thereby validating female contributions to the African American heritage. Afrocentrists have maintained that the legacy of our forefathers and foremothers (but primarily the forefathers) offer paradigms for living.

People like Marcus Garvey, W. E. B. DuBois, and Harriet Tubman are enlisted as role models of African American identity. Womanists critically examine the African American women whose lives are such that they, too, are role models. Womanists insist that African American women already have legitimate sources that articulate the struggles of African American women, even though they have been overlooked and underutilized as resources. This challenges the male-dominated Afrocentric dimension of our struggle. Womanists believe that we ourselves must decide what constitutes our experience. We must advance our own cause. We must uncover the voices of our mothers and grandmothers and foremothers. African American women must define who we are. This thinking, this doing, is both womanist and Afrocentric. Womanists incorporate information left by our female ancestors as primary resources for uncovering the strength and richness already present in the experience of African American women. We must name who we are, what we mean, and what we stand for. This process is both womanist and Afrocentric. Womanism is Afrocentric in its focus on African American women.

Dueling Ideologies?

An important Afrocentric concept is *Njia*, the ideology of victorious thought.[4] *Njia* celebrates the survival of African Americans who endured slavery and affirms the fact that the sons and daughters of slaves made significant contributions to the African American community. History is central to Afrocentrism because without an adequate understanding of our history we are doomed to accept definitions of ourselves that have been written by others. Both womanists and Afrocentrists denounce a reality imposed by others as invalid to our experience of the world. In both perspectives, the agenda for discussion is established by African Americans. Womanists and Afrocentrists confirm and affirm each other in declaring that we are our own best resource and that we must validate that which is ours—our writers, our historians, our scholars, our theologians. We must validate who we are on our own terms.

Sometimes the womanist and Afrocentric concepts merge, making clear distinction difficult. Womanism is Afrocentric, although Afrocentrism is not always womanist. In fact, the African American woman is minimally involved in the foundational precepts of the Afrocentric idea. Its language and images are predominantly male, and it does not evince an attempt to be inclusive.

The minimal presence of African American women in Afrocentrism points to an even greater need for the womanist perspective. The apparent lack of African American women in the conceptual framework of Afrocentrism is a continuation of their exclusion from dialogues about African Americans, a primary reason the womanist concept emerged. Womanists go beyond Afrocentrists because womanists call for a process that considers the health and wholeness of the entire community.[5] Womanists are concerned with building and maintaining the entire African American community—no one is excluded from the dialogue.[6] Womanists envision a community of African Americans who are working for the healing of everyone. For this to occur, womanists recognize, there must be open and honest discussion between African American men and women.

The essence of womanist thought is the healthy affirmation of African American women so that the entire African American community can survive, thrive, and become a vital force in the life of our people. Implicit in the womanist perspective is the idea that African American women have something to offer the community that has been heretofore overlooked or dismissed. Differences between womanism and Afrocentrism are, at root, ideological, and each has a distinct point of departure for engaging in dialogue. Womanists begin with the most oppressed group in the African American community, African American women. As Jacquelyn Grant has explained, African American women experience the "tridimensional oppression" of race, sex, and class; thus, full human liberation cannot be achieved simply by eliminating any one form of oppression.[7] Afrocentrists may be overlooking a great resource for enhancing the concepts of self-determination by minimizing the contributions of African American women in the cause of freedom and liberation of African Americans. Afrocentrists continue to perpetrate a patriarchal vision of the African American community. Patriarchy assumes male superiority at birth, a notion which fosters and upholds the oppression of women and children, especially female children. This philosophical stance is counterproductive and divisive; it calls for separation and hierarchy instead of mutuality, health, and wholeness in the community. Our community cannot afford to continue to exclude African American women from the dialogue about itself. Everyone is needed if we are going to survive as a people. While Afrocentrists seem to adopt patriarchy without critically examining its usefulness in the African American community, womanists challenge the traditional view of relational patterns by calling for a critical analysis of the African American community.

To survive, we must also examine the *manner* in which we relate in our community. We cannot afford to continue dysfunctional relational patterns. Patriarchy is destructive to both men and women, a false perspective that has cultivated an environment in which violence, oppression, and the dehumanization of women and children run rampant. Womanists challenge the patriarchal Afrocentrists. Patriarchy is paternal-

istic, and implies the superiority of one group, and its right to
dominate and rule; but we must be concerned about the entire
community.

Jarena Lee's In-Spite-Of Faith

Womanists further exemplify the Afrocentric idea or concept
by authenticating an "in-spite-of" faith. The African American
woman has survived and thrived in spite of often being ignored, excluded, and dismissed in the religious, theological,
and academic community. This in-spite-of faith was the essence of the life of Jarena Lee (b. 1783) a nineteenth-century
womanist who preached in spite of prohibitions and lack of
recognition from the church. Jarena Lee was both womanist
and Afrocentric in orientation because she refused to accept
the definitions of ministry that were imposed on her by society and by the African American church. She refused to define
herself in traditional definitions of the role of a woman. She
refused to ignore the reality of her own call in order to accom-
modate the ethos of her church and community. When Jarena
Lee approached Richard Allen regarding her call to the ministry, he dismissed her by stating that the Methodist discipline
made no provision for women to preach. Jarena Lee responded, "O how careful ought we to be lest through our by-
laws of church government and discipline, we bring into
disrepute even the work of life. . . . It should be remembered
that nothing is impossible with God."[8] Jarena Lee defined her
own ministry and thereby created a place for herself in the
world.

Jarena Lee "chose the better part"[9] and preached, although several attempts were made to silence her. She
preached in a century in which women were denied basic
human rights. A brief examination of the life of Jarena Lee will

reveal that she was a womanist and Afrocentric. As such, her life can be used as a role model for twentieth-century African American women struggling with the call of God upon their lives. Jarena Lee challenged the notion that only men could serve as preachers in the church of Christ:

> If a man may preach, because the Savior died for him, why not the woman? seeing he died for her also. Is he not a whole Savior, instead of a half one? As those who hold it wrong for a woman to preach would make it appear.[10]

With courage, boldness, and tenacity, Jarena Lee created a place for her ministry in spite of the prohibitions by her denomination and those in society. In so doing she has created a legacy of hope and inspiration that is the essence of womanist thought and Afrocentrism.

What compelled Jarena Lee to embrace the life of a gospel preacher in the face of discrimination and rejection? This compulsion is described by Cheryl Townsend Gilkes's statement regarding the "holy boldness" of women who casually remind us that if it were not for the church women we would not have a church.[11] It is also included in what Sheila Briggs calls "a radical commitment to be obedient," which involves a woman knowing why she is doing something.[12] Katie G. Cannon would call it "unctuousness," which is the quality of steadfastness akin to fortitude in the face of formidable oppression,[13] or "liberationist," in which "one challenges and reshapes the traditional inquiry and raises candid questions."[14] The above characteristics are reflected in the life of Jarena Lee as she struggled to establish her identity as a called gospel preacher in the nineteenth century. These characteristics are also reflected in womanists who challenge traditions that exclude women from dialogue or participation in various arenas on the basis of gender.

The fact that Jarena Lee preached is undisputed. Why she preached may be instructive for African American women who continue to confront a structure that denies the authenticity of the female voice, in both church and society, in the role of preaching the gospel of Jesus Christ. Jarena Lee says she preached in the face of oppression and reproach because she was compelled to do so. She states:

> as for me, I am fully persuaded that the Lord called me to labor according to what I received, in his vineyard. If he has not, how could he consistently bear testimony in favor of my poor labors, awakening and converting sinners?[15]

Jarena Lee's life is worthy of our examination and reflection because her life as an African American female preacher may provide a paradigm for African American female preachers today. As we continue to listen to the voice that speaks in the stillness of our moments, we need to know that other African American women have had the same experience and survived. Having this knowledge of our foremothers and forefathers provides a legacy of faith in-spite-of and struggle in-spite-of that can still allow African American women called to ministry to "mount up with wings like eagles, [to] run and not be weary, [and to] walk and not faint."[16]

Jarena Lee chose not to accept the prohibitions against women preaching which indicates that she was Afrocentric in orientation. That is, she would not allow the prohibitions against her to deter her from her call. She asks, "and why should it be thought impossible, heterodox, or improper for a woman to preach, seeing the Savior died for the woman as well as the man?"[17]

One of the distinctive elements of Afrocentrism is "intelligence and boldness,"[18] that is, going against traditions that impose a foreign reality that contradicts our own. Jarena Lee boldly asserted her right to define herself and her understanding of God. She was both a womanist and an Afrocentrist. The life of Jarena Lee certainly reflects her commitment to the struggle for freedom of self-expression. Her experience continues to inform us preaching women about who we are and who we can become.

Jarena Lee left a journal of her encounter with this nineteenth-century community to instruct other African American women about her journey of faith. She left a legacy of in-spite-of faith because she remained true to the call of God that she knew to be hers. Without wavering or apologizing, she established a place for her ministry. She challenged sexism and patriarchy by preaching regardless. In her words, "Mary first preached the risen Saviour, and is not the doctrine of the resurrection the climax of Christianity?"[19] As a nineteenth-century womanist, "she loved the spirit, loved the struggle, loved the folk and loved herself, regardless."[20] In embracing self-love and love of her people, Lee challenged the notion that ministry was a male preserve. She refused to accept a reality that on the basis of her gender alone denied her right to exist and express herself. She refused to accept a reality that suggested that she was inferior because of her gender; in fact she challenged those who questioned her call to authenticate their objections in God's word. She refused to accept "man-made" definitions of women. Jarena Lee was bold, tenacious, courageous, and self-affirming, all central components of both womanism and Afrocentrism.

4

To Reflect the Image of God

A Womanist Perspective on Right Relationship

◆◆◆◆◆◆◆◆◆◆◆◆◆◆◆◆◆◆◆◆◆◆◆◆◆◆◆◆◆◆◆◆◆

Kelly Brown Douglas

A Community in Crisis

A womanist is "committed to survival and wholeness of entire people, male *and* female."[1] It is this womanist commitment that compels us into dialogue with black male theologians and religious scholars. A significant segment of our community — our girls and boys, our women and men — are caught in a spiral of death and brokenness. They too often succumb to the crime, drugs, disease, lack of life- and freedom-producing values, that an "interlocking system" of multiple oppression — that is, racism, sexism, poverty, and heterosexism — breeds.[2] If theologians are faithful to God's task of bringing God's creatures to "the beloved community," and if theologians are to formulate any meaningful response to the crisis that currently engulfs our community, then this is only one of many crucial dialogues. Men need to talk to men, women need to talk unapologetically to women. Womanist and black male theologians must begin the discussion.

The crisis in our community demands that this time together be more than simply a discussion of the sin of sexism. In fact, the womanist challenge, too, involves more than this one-dimensional focus. The crisis of our people, as well as the womanist concept, calls us to explore forthrightly what it means for African American women and men to be in "right relationship" with one another. That is, to be in the kind of relationship that promotes "survival and wholeness for entire people, male and female." What is meant by wholeness? Wholeness first implies an individual's triumph over her or his wounds of oppression, so that the individual is whole even as she or he struggles for the community's wholeness. Second, wholeness for a community indicates that it is not divided against itself and that it is free, liberated from oppression. This chapter will offer a womanist perspective on relationships of life and wholeness for the African American community.

The Enslaved Women's Culture of Resistance

Cheryl Townsend Gilkes aptly observes that the womanist concept is one that "lays out very clear positions that Black women ought to adopt based upon the best traditions ingrained in their legacy of struggle, survival, and the construction of African-American women's culture."[3] A particular tradition of struggle to which the womanist concept draws us emerged during slavery. Enslaved women responded to the hideously inhumane circumstances of slavery by forging what Patricia Collins calls a "culture of resistance." This culture was crafted and nurtured largely in the enslaved quarters. These quarters became for enslaved women what Collins identifies as "contradictory locations," that is, spaces in the midst of oppression that "simultaneously confine yet allow Black women to develop cultures of resistance."[4] An essential part of the enslaved female's culture of resistance, which challenges the way womanists do theology, is the relationships which enslaved women formed with their families and their men. These relationships were critical to frustrating the daily attacks on the enslaved community's humanity. They were instrumental in the survival and wholeness of enslaved women and men, enslaved girls and boys. This, what might be termed a womanist way of relating in the enslaved community, begins with a particular notion of family.

The enslaved women's view of family was grounded in their West African tradition of family as "extended kin units."[5] While in West Africa familial relationships were carefully monitored by bloodlines, in enslaved communities they were broadened. Essentially, the enslaved African transformed the notion of bloodlines into one of blood, whereby anyone with African blood was considered family. Such an understanding of family included the entire enslaved community. So the enslaved Africans saw themselves as members of one family — the community was family and the family was community. This family/community concept served to foster unity within the slave quarters. It affirmed for enslaved women as well as for enslaved men the necessity of "group" survival. If the family was to survive, the group had to survive, and responsibility to the family was also responsibility to the group. This model had significant implications for the enslaved woman's particular relationships.

During slavery African women maintained what was their primary and most significant relationship in West Africa: their bond with their children. Of course, the slave system brutally exploited this role of mother. Enslaved women, for instance, were made the "mammies" of their masters' and mistresses' children. But in the contradictory location of the enslaved quarters, the relationship between mother and child was an indispensable component of the enslaved family/community's survival.

The enslaved woman cared for and nurtured the children. Even in the face of enormous odds, she was the one who provided for their daily needs, such as food and clothing. Many enslaved women carried their nursing children with them on their backs to the field as evidenced in a testimony that describes an enslaved women carrying her infant in a knapsack fastened upon her back.[6] Another testimony tells of an enslaved mother who stayed up after the others had gone to bed to sew and mend her children's clothes:

> She would not get through to go to her log cabin until nine or ten o'clock at night. She would then be so tired that she could scarcely stand; but she would find one boy with his knee out, and another with his elbow out, a patch wanting here, and a stitch there, and she would sit down by her lightwood fire, and sew and sleep alternately.[7]

The enslaved woman was also the central purveyor of cultural and religious values to her children. As one enslaved male remembered his mother, "She always tried to do right, and taught her children to know right from wrong. When I was a little child, she taught me to know my Maker, and that we should all die, and if we were good, we should be happy."[8]

Given the definition of family that existed in the enslaved community, coupled with the exigencies of slavery, enslaved women were frequently "mothers" to children that were not biologically their own. When biological mothers were separated from their children by sale or death, "other mothers" would step in to care for the children left behind. When the daily demands of slavery took a mother away from her child, "other mothers" would care for that son or daughter. This concept of "other mothers" was also present in West African women's culture. In the slave community, regardless of the condition of the biological mother, there was no child without a mother. As one testimony witnesses: "Among the slave children were three little orphans, whose mothers, at their death, committed them to the care of my mother. One of them was a babe. She took them and treated them as her own."[9]

To be a mother in West Africa was also to perform more than the "traditional" domestic duties of caring for children. The role of motherhood in West Africa often took the woman into the marketplace or onto the farm. The West African woman was accustomed to labor outside the home as an essential part of her position as caretaker of her children and family. Again, the slavocracy exploited this aspect of the African woman's life as it assigned her to the same brutal and harsh tasks it foisted on the African man. Yet, if the slavocracy made little distinction between the labor of enslaved women and enslaved men, in the slave quarters a distinction was made.

It was in the quarters that enslaved women were able to create a protected space and therefore forge an identity, as well as a relationship with their men that would best enhance their survival and wholeness as well as that of their families. Within the quarters the enslaved female was responsible primarily for the domestic chores, which included caring for the children, cooking, cleaning, sewing, etc. The enslaved male/husband was responsible for the chores outside of the quarters; this might include gardening, fishing, hunting, etc.

While historian Deborah Gray White astutely points out that it is not at all clear how the enslaved female felt about her domestic work, especially given that she was often up to complete her duties long after the men had retired, one thing is clear: the specified female world allowed for networking and strong bonds between enslaved women. This networking often involved cooperation in the work of the quarters as well as the fields, cooperative child care, and impromptu religious services. It no doubt fostered intimacy between the women.[10] Essentially, this kind of female-male delineation of family responsibility was to some degree freeing for the enslaved woman. It represented a form of resistance to the indignities of slavery. It defied the gender-neutral way in which slavemasters viewed enslaved women's labor. It was a way for the enslaved female to define for herself what it meant to be a woman. It should be noted that there were times when the wife had to carry forth the male role in the quarters. This occurred as enslaved women were involved in "abroad marriages," i.e., marriages to someone on a different plantation, or when their husbands escaped slavery, were sold away, or were dead.

Equally significant, in spite of the clear distinctions between women's and men's work in the slaves' quarters, there was apparently no belief in inequality. While the role and function of enslaved women and men were decidedly different in their quarters, one role was not considered more or less important than the other. They were considered equally essential to the survival and wholeness of the enslaved family/community. Enslaved women and men related to each other as equals. They engaged in complementary and reciprocal relationships. Any other kinds of relationships probably would have proven disastrous for the life and well-being of their sons and daughters, as well as for themselves. Indeed, several historians have noted the unusual equality between women and men, wives and husbands in the enslaved community. Historian Jacqueline Jones observes:

Within well-defined limits, the slaves created — or pre-
served — an explicit sexual division of labor based on their
own preferences. Husbands and wives and fathers and
mothers had reciprocal obligations toward one another.
Together they worked to preserve the integrity of the
family. . . . Relations between the sexes approximated a
"healthy sexual equality."[11]

White perhaps best captures the significance of the relationships between enslaved women and men when she says:

Slave families were unusually egalitarian. Equality could
not have been based on sameness because, while slave
men and women often did the same kinds of work and
provided similar services, many jobs and responsibilities
still belonged by definition to one sex or other. This suggests that equality within the slave family was founded on
complementary roles, roles that were different yet so
critical to slave survival that they were of equal necessity.[12]

A Womanist Way of Relating

In a manner integral to the struggle for the survival and wholeness of enslaved women and men, girls and boys, enslaved
women adopted what might be termed a womanist way of relating to their families and men. This involved: (1) a community understanding of family, (2) a willingness to do what was
necessary for the well-being of the family/community, (3)
female networking and cooperation, and (4) a reciprocal relationship of equality and respect with their men/husbands.

What does this way of relating as it emerged in enslaved
women's culture suggest for us as womanist black theologians
and religious scholars committed to the survival and wholeness of our community? First, we are urged to make a concern

for family central to our work. In so doing we are challenged to move African American men and women, and our black church congregations, back to the mode of family as community. This means that our theologies must engage in the kinds of analyses that confront the interlocking system of oppression that prevents our community from being whole, from being family. Therefore we must oppose the complexity of racism, sexism, classism, and heterosexism not only as it impinges upon the African American community, but also as it sets the community against itself. The family/community concept necessitates a social-political analysis that prompts the elimination of the "us vs. them" mentality, which is too often present within our community and its churches when we discuss issues of complexion, gender, economic status, or sexual preference. Our survival and wholeness demand that every member of the African American community be accepted as a member of the family and treated and cared for accordingly. Our theologies must make clear that our churches, for instance, are compelled to respond to those persons most victimized by the crime, drugs, and disease that the interlocking system of racism, sexism, classism, and heterosexism breeds. As members of the African American family/community we have responsibility for and to each other. Most importantly, our theologies must clarify that if one member of the family is not whole, the entire family/community is not free.

Second, the womanist way of relating that was born in enslaved women's culture demands that women and men be free to shape their own identities and to choose their own roles in the African American family/community's fight for survival and wholeness. It requires that our theologies embrace a religious and cultural analysis that critiques any aspect of African American religion and culture that limits a person's freedom to participate at every level and capacity in the church and community. This analysis must also challenge any notion of a divinely sanctioned order or hierarchy that restricts a person to a particular role or function in the family/community or church because of their gender or sexual preference. Such an analysis should attest that the care and nurturing of children is a community task, the responsibility of both men and women. It should disavow any notion that childcare is a woman's duty, as opposed to a choice she can make. At the same time, such an analysis must free the community from restrictive ideologies about the nature of households and who can raise children. This analysis must affirm households of women, or men, as well as households of single women or single men who foster the life and wholeness of girls and boys. This religious and cultural analysis should further disavow any notion that only heterosexuals or heterosexual couples can raise and care for children.

Moreover, our theologies must be careful not to embrace or affirm language, models, movements, or ways of thinking that tend to limit people to certain roles based on gender or sexual preference. In this regard, a religious and cultural analysis might critique some of the manifestations of the Afrocentric movement that tend to foster sexist and homophobic ideologies. Essentially, the womanist way of relating in the enslaved quarters challenges us to adopt the kind of religious and cultural analysis that would empower persons to do what they are willing to do to promote the survival and wholeness of the African American family/community.

Finally, perhaps the most significant aspect of the enslaved women's relationships was that they were reciprocal relationships of mutuality, especially those with their men. In this regard, we are challenged to promote and model for our churches and community these types of complementary, equal relationships between persons in our family/community. We must move our churches, for instance, away from hierarchical models of leadership which typically relegate women to positions considered less significant. Our theologies must make clear that no person—regardless of color, gender, economic status, or sexual preference—or task is of more or less value in the struggle for the community's survival and wholeness.

Womanist Reflections of the Image of God

The womanist way of relating fosters life and wholeness for the African American community, even as the community struggles for these precise goals in the face of an interlocking system of multidimensional oppression. That fact may be enough to compel us to incorporate such a way of relating into our theological analysis. But the question that we as theologians are at some point obliged to ask is, What has this to do with God?

To be sure, the religion of enslaved women affirmed the presence of God in their efforts to promote life and wholeness for themselves and their families. There is perhaps no more poignant witness to this than Sojourner Truth's powerful testimony after losing most of her thirteen children to the slave system: "I cried out my mother's grief and none but Jesus heard me!"[13] Various womanist writings have indeed pointed out that the God of the Hebrew midwives, the God of the prophets, and the God of Jesus Christ is a God of survival and wholeness. But a womanist way of relating is indicative of something more than this aspect of who God is and God's call to us.

In spite of the confusion perhaps inherent in the doctrine, as well as the sexist and homophobic images which feminist theologians have aptly shown that the doctrine promotes, the trinitarian understanding (which I confess is becoming in-

creasingly significant to my own Christian beliefs) suggests
something crucial about God. It attests that the God of life
and wholeness is a God who is internally and eternally relational. For us then to reflect what it means to be in the image
of God, is for us to be in relationship. Further, we are called by
the image of God which is ours to reflect, to be in particular
kinds of relationships. Enslaved women and men testified to
these relationships as they encountered God in their struggle
for life and wholeness. Their religion, while recognizing the
different functions of God the Creator, Jesus, and the Spirit,
appeared often to make little distinction between them. God
and Jesus, especially, are seen as one. This was perhaps enslaved women's and men's way of testifying to the fact that
though their roles are different, God, Jesus, and even the Spirit
are of profoundly equal significance as they sustain and empower them in their struggle. Challenged by the faith of the
enslaved Africans, to be in the image of God is for us to be in
relationships of mutuality as we strive for life and wholeness.
In this regard, as enslaved women nurtured a womanist way of
relating to their families and especially their men, they were
reflecting what it meant for them to have been created in the
image of God.

The African American community faces a crisis, perhaps
best described by the word *genocide*. It is our duty as African
American women and men doing theology to help to forge a
culture of resistance that will promote life and wholeness for
the entire community—even as we struggle to dismantle the
interlocking system of multidimensional oppression. In so
doing, we are called to a womanist way of relating to the community and with each other. The crisis of our community
compels us to be to our community the image of God who is
life and wholeness.

PART ◇ TWO
INTERPRETATION

5

Slavery as a Sacred Text

Witnessing in *Dessa Rose*

◆◆◆◆◆◆◆◆◆◆◆◆◆◆◆◆◆◆◆◆◆◆◆◆◆◆◆◆◆◆◆◆◆

Deborah E. McDowell

How could she bear witness to what she'd never lived?
Gayl Jones
Corregidora

History is "cannibalistic," and memory becomes the
closed arena of conflict between two contradictory operations: forgetting, an action directed against the past,
and the return of what was forgotten.
Michel de Certeau
Heterologies: Discourses on the Other

*I*nitially, this inquiry was
guided by two related questions. The first question was, What
notions of God are present in literature by black women? and
the second, What does Scripture mean to them? Not surprisingly, random examples suggest that answers to both questions are complex, historically contingent, and variable. Even
in those works in which God has been imaged as, to borrow
from Alice Walker's *The Color Purple*, "big and old and tall and
graybearded and white,"[1] the thematic insistence on female
self-determination has been fundamental and strong. In *The
Life and Spiritual Experiences of Jarena Lee* (1836), for example,
a spiritual autobiography that inaugurated the genre for black
women, Jarena Lee "gives an account of her call to preach the

gospel."[2] Challenging those who considered it unseemly for her to do so, Lee questions, "If a man may preach, because the Savior died for him, why not the woman? seeing he died for her also. Is he not a whole Savior, instead of a half one? Did not Mary, a woman, preach the gospel?" Anticipating resistance, Lee continues: "But some will say that Mary did not expound the Scripture, [and] therefore, she did not preach, in the proper sense of the term. To this I reply, it may be that the term *preach* . . . did not mean exactly what it is now *made* to mean."[3] I will return to Jarena Lee's implicit defense of the historical contingencies of discourse.

Two works written in the late twentieth century offering more radical notions of God and conjoined with themes of female self-determination are Ntozake Shange's *for colored girls who have considered suicide when the rainbow is enuf* (1980) and Alice Walker's *The Color Purple* (1982). It should come as no surprise that these books, in some circles, have been roundly excoriated and branded as subversive. The rainbow in Shange's title, suggesting the mythic covenant between God and Noah, symbolizes hope and the promise of a new life in which God is reimagined as mother and resides in the self. In *The Color Purple*, as Delores Williams has so astutely observed, God is divinity without gender, neither male nor female, but a spirit dwelling in everyone and everything.[4]

Turning to the second question, what Scripture means to black women, it seems that it means different things at different times to different writers. Scripture is not sacred as an untamperable given; it is rather a set of texts to be questioned, negotiated with, and variously interpreted. Among contemporary black female novelists, perhaps Toni Morrison demonstrates this most boldly. Anyone who has read *Song of Solomon* readily notes the liberties taken not only with that "sacred text," but also with other aspects of Scripture, especially the first (Christian) names of the Dead family: First Corinthians

Dead; Magdalene, called Lena Dead; and most audacious,
Pilate Dead, whose name was copied from the Bible by her illiterate father. When the midwife protests, "You can't name
the baby this," he commands her, "Say it." She answers,
"Pilate." He asks, "Like a riverboat pilot?" She says no, "Like
a Christ-killing Pilate. You can't get much worse than that for
a name, and a baby girl at that."[5] Literature is replete with ir-
reverent representations of sacred texts.

My approach to the topic in this chapter is not in keeping
with my strong background in black women's literature, or
stretching and transforming texts and terms for their own purposes; instead, I want to be as "free" in interpreting the *concept*
of sacred texts as black women writers have been. I will redefine this concept in order to examine a nonbiblical "sacred
text," one that its apologists have finally defended by invoking
and insisting on the authority of the Bible. This sacred text is
slavery.

I am aware that the idea of slavery as sacred text creates
something of a paradox, for *sacred* evokes ideas of the holy, the
hallowed, and the consecrated that are not easily reconciled
with what the utterance of the word *slavery* almost always
evokes: unfathomable and dehumanizing brutalities inflicted
on a people for hundreds of years. While I acknowledge this
seeming paradox, I would like to pursue it in order to reflect
on slavery as sacred text to African American writers.

Some definitions are in order. Adapting M. M. Bakhtin's
definition of authoritative discourse, I am defining a "sacred
text" as "privileged language that approaches us from without," language that is "distanced [and] permits no play with its
framing context. . . . We recite it. It has great power over us."[6]
Opposed to the language of the sacred text is what Bakhtin
calls "internally persuasive discourse . . . which is more akin to
retelling a text in one's own words, with one's own accents,
gestures, modifications." We must struggle, he concludes, be-

tween these two types of discourse, assimilating but also simultaneously "freeing" one's own "discourse from the
authoritative word."[7]

Freeing their discourse from the authoritative word is an
act quite common among African American writers, and the
women writers of this tradition are especially good at it. Finding their own words in the sprawling discourse on slavery is a
challenge that black writers—male and female—have confronted at various cycles of their history, beginning with the
slave narratives, which are regarded by many students of the
genre as "culture-defining scripture."[8]

Judging from the flood of recent novels about slavery by
African Americans, Ralph Ellison was not amiss in remarking
that "the Negro American consciousness is not a product of a
will to historical forgetfulness."[9] Yet this has not always been
the case. The emergence of what Bernard Bell calls "neoslave
narratives"[10] is mainly a post-1960s phenomenon.[11] Margaret
Walker's *Jubilee* can be seen as something of a catalyst because,
since its publication in 1966, novels about slavery have appeared at a prodigious rate.[12] Why the compulsion to repeat
the massive story of slavery in the contemporary African
American novel, especially so long after the event itself, after
the fact of slavery? Is it simply because contemporary writers
can "witness" slavery from the "safe" vantage point of 100
years' distance? What personal need, what expressive function,
does representing slavery in narrative serve the twentieth-century African American writer? Is the retelling meant to attempt the impossible—to get it right, set the record straight?

However one chooses to answer these questions, it is certain that recent fictionalizations of slavery insert themselves—
some by explicit design—into the store of warring texts and
conflicting interpretations of chattel slavery.[13] Margaret
Walker admits that her motivation for writing *Jubilee* was "to
set the record straight where Black people are concerned in

terms of the Civil War, of slavery, segregation and Reconstruction."[14]

Like Walker, Sherley Anne Williams suggests that history's lies can be corrected and its omissions restored. In the Author's Note to her novel *Dessa Rose*, Williams admits to "being outraged by a certain, critically acclaimed novel . . . that travestied the as-told-to memoir of slave revolt leader Nat Turner."[15] Here she refers to William Styron's controversial novel *Confessions of Nat Turner* (1967),[16] whose "meditation on history"[17] is an example of what Williams, in her preface, considers the betrayal of blacks by the written word. Her outrage is understandable considering the repeated scene of blacks' erasure *from* the historical record and their misrepresentation *in* it. But while Williams's "Author's Note" explicitly critiques a novel that allegedly takes history lightly and misrepresents the "known facts" about a black hero, it licenses itself to do much the same: to invent and re-create history. Williams takes two different documented stories, one involving a pregnant black woman who helped to lead a slave revolt in Kentucky, and the other about a white woman in North Carolina who reportedly gave sanctuary to runaway slaves. Thinking it "sad . . . that these two women never met," Williams, in fact, brings them together in fiction. Does Williams's preface reveal a flagrant literary double standard concerning the uses of history in fiction? Does it suggest that it is all right for one writer to take liberties with history and not another? I don't think so.

Dessa Rose stages multiple, often contradictory versions of Dessa's enslavement and subsequent escape, which underscore well-rehearsed and commonplace assumptions about the difficulty, if not the impossibility, of ascertaining Truth. Yet the novel is straightforward and unambiguous in its assertion that some versions come closer than others in acquiring the force of truth, marking it as a resolutely propositional and polemical novel. It confronts unabashedly the inescapably ideological contingencies of all discourse, itself included. Exposed in the telling of Dessa's story is a complex and shifting web of social and historical realities involved in representing slavery. The novel asks implicitly: Who has been historically authorized, or, who have authorized themselves, to tell the story and under what circumstances? What has been acceptably sayable about that story? How have black women figured in it or figured themselves in it?

It is well known that the majority of published slave narratives were written by black men. According to John Blassingame, black women wrote less than 12 percent of the published slave narratives.[18] This statistic shows the slave narratives' status as autobiography to be the expression of male subjectivity, and their status as history to be *his* story. When black women have figured in these narratives, they appear largely as victims of sexual abuse.[19] Significantly, the majority of contemporary novels about slavery have been written by black women, and thus it might be argued that these novels reclaim a female-gendered subjectivity more complex in dimension that dramatizes not what was *done* to slave women, but what they *did* with what was done to them. Removing the stress points of this story from passive victimization to creative agency can be considered analogous to substituting new words for and in a sacred text.

Concerns about the who, what, when, and how of slave narratives are richly suggestive and resonate far beyond the imagined scene of the institution that ended in the nineteenth century. This is, to be sure, not a surprising observation, considering that what we call the past is merely a function and production of the present and its discourses. We might even argue that it is precisely the "present" and its discourses that *Dessa Rose* confronts. To choose arbitrarily from its diversely textured field, we can say that the novel raises questions about, comments on, agrees with, and explicitly challenges many issues at the forefront of the hydra-headed enterprise—some would say monster—that we loosely term "contemporary critical discourse."

Williams's novel participates aggressively in the critique of both the subject and binary opposites, which are commonly associated with the poststructuralist project. With equal vigor, the novel wrestles with questions about the politics and problems of language and representation. But *Dessa Rose* swerves away from the empty notions of radical indeterminacy that have become the trademark of so much of the discourse at the center of the contemporary critical stage.

It swerves in grounding the oppositions it stages—slavery and freedom, orality and literacy, fact and fiction—in an untidy network of social and material specificities. We might say, finally, that in telling the story of a woman's passage from slavery to freedom, the novel negotiates between past and present to reveal, not surprisingly, that they are not at all discrete. Clearly, her passage is, after all, not a progressive evolution from slavery to freedom, for slavery's effects linger long after she has escaped its physical hold. Correspondingly, from the novel I take my license as a reader to negotiate between the "past" and "present" tenses of critical discourse, because I want both to "master" the text by telling it and to free it to tell itself, to return the text to the world of concrete reality and to insist that that realm is only a world of words.

I

I know this darky, I tell you; I know her very well.

Nehemiah, *Dessa Rose*

Just whose word can and should be taken in *Dessa Rose* is
a preoccupying question of the novel in its multiple versions of
Dessa's life as a slave. A continuous thread of quotation marks
woven throughout the text calls attention to words as words
that evoke uncertainty and ambiguity. But more than that,
these repetitive quotation marks mark separate, enclosed
words set apart from the discourse of the implied author. But
while the different versions of Dessa's story point to the fact
that the "true" story is difficult to ascertain, the novel resists
the pull of the postmodern orthodoxy of indecisiveness and
relativism. In other words, while there might not be one
"truth" about Dessa (or about slavery, more generally), there
are "certainties" that the text stubbornly claims and validates
and those it subverts.

The first recorded version of Dessa's story comes from
the aptly named Adam (namer) Nehemiah (chronicler), whose
"authority" as an agent of white male law and rationality is aggressively undermined by the text. In creating Nehemiah, Williams parodies the "as-told-to" device of gathering empirical
evidence and documenting events to construct historicist discourse. Nehemiah is supposedly collecting the facts of Dessa's
unrepentant participation in a slave revolt in which many
whites were killed. The "facts" that he collects, however, are
"some kind of fantastical fiction" (39), re-created in his hand.

The novel compounds the ironies and limitations inherent in Nehemiah's account, which is suspect from the start. It
is retrospective, based on discrepant sources, and recon-
structed from notes. First, though it purports to be about
Dessa, a particular slave woman, Nehemiah's account actually

essentializes Dessa and attempts to fit her into a recognizably proslavery text. His representation is culled from an inherited store of racist myths about slaves and slavery. "He had been told [slaves] fell asleep much as a cow would in the midst of a satisfying chew. . . . He had not observed this himself" (36). And, throughout his chronicle, which is significantly entitled "Darky," a generic, gender-neutral classification of slaves, Nehemiah admits to being unable to "remember [Dessa's] name" (45). Failing to remember it, he performs a series of substitutions that are also lifted from the standard vocabulary of the proslavery text: "darky," "fiend," "devil-woman," "treacherous nigger bitch," "virago," and "she-devil." Although Nehemiah takes notes on the names of slaves that Dessa refers to in her reveries, in his translation they are all reduced to "darky" (39).

Nehemiah's colossal act of serial misnaming mistakes the name for the thing or, to borrow from Kimberly Benston, it "subsume[s] the complexities of human experience into a tractable sign while manifesting an essential inability to *see* (to grasp, to apprehend) the signified."[20] In telling Dessa's story, Nehemiah creates an abstraction and assigns it a place distant from himself, a distance structured in the use of architectural space (place) and somatophobic imagery. Although Nehemiah conducts his first meeting with Dessa in the root cellar that is her jail, he decides that being "closeted with the darky within the small confines of the cellar was an unsettling experience" (23), and so he holds subsequent meetings outdoors where she can be kept at a distance from him. Outside, "he kept a careful distance between them," "sitting above and behind her . . . he would lean forward long enough to wave her to a spot several feet from him, using the vinegar-soaked handkerchief . . . meant to protect him from her scent" (56). These vertical images of inside and outside, up and down (he is *up* in the attic of Hughes's farmhouse; she is outside it and *down* in the root cellar),[21] and images of smell maintain the distance between Dessa and Nehemiah that contributes to his inability to see and to name her.

Hoping to ensure the continued circulation of these performative misnamings and descriptions, Nehemiah is at work on a book on the origins of uprisings among slaves. Commissioned by his publisher, Browning Norton, Nehemiah's projected book, *The Roots of Rebellion in the Slave Population and Some Means of Eradicating Them*, exposes his project as a form of slave trading, or trading in words, and as a tool in the technocratic machinery (he is the son of a mechanic) of social control. But this is no simple story of a black women's total victimization by that machinery, since Nehemiah proves no match for Dessa.

The narrative symmetrically opposes Nehemiah's public discourse to Dessa's poignant expressions of personal loss and longing. For every question he wants answered with facts about the uprising—"Where were the renegades going?" "Who were the darkies that got away?" (36)—Dessa answers with some memory of her lover Kaine's confrontation with the slave system or by singing a song. Throughout their sessions, she cleverly misleads him and mocks what he represents. And in the studied circularity of her telling, leading Nehemiah back to the same point of previous sessions and her skill at "turn-[ing] his . . . questions back upon themselves," Dessa sabotages his enterprise. Her confessed enjoyment of "play[ing] on his words" sends him scrambling to write "quickly, abbreviating with a reckless abandon, scribbling almost as he sought to keep up with the flow of her words" (60). Her refusal to "confess" anything to Nehemiah that would facilitate yet another misrepresentation is an act of resistance against the adverse power of literacy and codification. At novel's end, Nehemiah's "book" is incomplete; it has literally fallen apart and is nothing more than loose pages "scatter[ed] about the floor," unreadable scribble that even the sheriff, who is another agent of the father's law, cannot read. Further, Nehemiah's own name has been abbreviated; he is "Nemi" and has become the reduction he would create.

II

The evidence of things not seen.

Hebrews 11:1

Can we identify a work of art . . . if it does not bear the mark of a genre?

Jacques Derrida
"The Law of Genre"

A point graphically illustrated in section two of *Dessa Rose* is that misnaming is generative. In escaping from Nehemiah, Dessa seizes physical freedom, but she does not escape the text of slavery. She continues to be misnamed and performs her own misnaming. We might say that sections one and two juxtapose two consubstantial systems of representation—one is verbal, the other visual. Told largely from the point of view of Rufel, a white woman, this second section is structured on the language of the visual that she employs while remembering her own past and her own complicity in and victimization by the institution of slavery.

Whereas the first section is based on a series of oppositions—of orality and literacy, public and private discourse, or a free white male and an enslaved black woman— the second questions "the whole business of choosing sides" (78), and moves toward an ethic and an energy of cooperation. That ethic is most readily apparent in the links established between Dessa and Rufel, an escaped slave and a onetime slave mistress, respectively. Both are separated from their

families, mourning personal losses, raising children, and living
under a system that denies each of them control over their
bodies. But these common denominators are produced by
radically different material circumstances and thus engender
radically different effects. While Rufel's section uses the problem of naming and representation to attempt to bridge the
"schism in the sisterhood,"[22] between black and white
women, it neither abbreviates and simplifies that process nor
attempts to merge their differences and make them the same.
It makes a difference that one woman is white and the other
black. Transgressing their oppositions, antagonisms, and the
impregnable social boundaries that separate them, begins with
efforts to get out of the text of slavery that both misnames and
"missees."

As slave mistress in action, Rufel replicates and extends
Nehemiah's practice of essentializing slaves and consigning
them to places. Whereas his section is entitled "Darky"—a
gender-neutral nomination—Rufel's is titled "Wench," a fe-
male-specific nomination, but one no closer to capturing
Dessa Rose. True to her trade as a caricaturist, Rufel has an
exaggerated and distorted image of Dessa and the other escaped slaves harbored on her rundown plantation, forcing
them into a visual mold produced and reproduced in nineteenth-century popular culture for ideological and proscriptive
purposes. In other words, she substitutes pictures for words.
Rufel associates Ada with "the stock cuts used to illustrate
newspaper advertisements of slave sales and runaways: pants
rolled up to the knees, bareheaded, a bundle attached to a stick
slung over one shoulder, the round white eyes in the inky face"
(140). Coming close upon Nathan at the shoreline, "she
turned to the darky aghast. . . . Never had she seen such blackness. She . . . expect[ed] to see the bulbous lips and bulging
eyes of a burnt-cork minstrel," but saw instead "a pair of rather
shadowy eyes and strongly defined features that were—

handsome" (125). Finally, as she remembers her faithful servant, Mammy, whose death she mourns, Rufel performs a
visual substitution extracted again from the text of slavery.
She starts to visualize Mammy's cream-colored bandanna, the traditional sign of the slave woman's servitude, but she corrects
that memory by recalling that "the silky-looking cloth on the
darky's head bore little resemblance to the gaudy-colored
swatch most darkies tied about their heads. This was a scarf,
knotted in a rosette behind one ear" (123). These passages
suggest that, while Rufel seems able to adjust her vision of
these slaves, she cannot right their names, not even Mammy,
the name of the slave woman she professes to love.

Significantly, it is over Rufel's misnaming Mammy that
she and Dessa have their first major confrontation, and their
mutual misnaming is a source of continual difficulty and mis-
trust. As Rufel fits Mammy into her largely idealized memo-
ries of her life as a Southern belle in Charleston, Dessa bursts
out, " 'Mammy' ain't nobody name, not they real one" (119).
Dessa forces Rufel to see that if she didn't know Mammy's
name, she didn't know Mammy. Even the most basic details
about Mammy are unknown to Rufel, who is left to wonder in
hindsight: "Had Mammy minded when the family no longer
called her name? . . . How old *had* Mammy been? . . . Had she
any children?" (129).

Though the confrontation between Rufel and Dessa over
"Mammy" is painful to them both, it puts each in touch with
the buried aspects of her past and initiates the process of intimacy and trust. That process figures into the poetics of space
and architecture. Whereas Nehemiah's section employs images
of vertical space to underscore the *distance* between him and
Dessa, Rufel uses images of horizontal space to figure the possibility of *closeness* between the two women.

Sutton's Glen is Rufel's down-at-the-heels plantation.
Its "Big House" consists of two large rooms and a lean-to

kitchen. Significantly, it has no second floor. The slave quarters consist of "one room with a dirt floor" (165), with one side for women and one for men (116). This spatial configuration is used to abrogate the hierarchies of place, the divisions in the social order that place Rufel at the top and Dessa below. Brought to Sutton's Glen weak and delirious from childbirth, Dessa is taken to Rufel's bedroom and placed in her bed. While the bed implies no necessary eroticism and becomes the symbolic site of mediation between these two women, only mutual acts of imagination and self-projection can bridge the chasm of mutual suspicion and distrust.

The burden of initiation falls largely on Rufel, who maintains a place of privilege and power despite her own victimization by the slave system. For example, according to the laws and customs governing Southern race relations, Rufel's word is equivalent to truth. As Ada says, "White woman ain't got no excuse to be trifling when all it take is they word" (176), a point made evident when Dessa is temporarily recaptured. It is Rufel's word, as a Southern Lady, even in the form of a disguise, that helps to free Dessa for the last time, underscoring Rufel's power over Dessa's life, her body, and her story.

While Rufel can shelter Dessa, she cannot believe that Dessa has been physically abused. Consistent with her penchant for the visual as well as her need for entertainment, Rufel wants to *hear* Dessa's story and *see* the visual "evidence," but Dessa, also suspicious, refuses to comply. The narrative that Rufel hears of Dessa's abuse is mediated, coming secondhand from Nathan. Rufel disbelieves the story because she sees no scars on Dessa's back. When Nathan explains that they are on her hips and thighs, Rufel asks, "How do you know?" Clearly, Rufel needs "to see them scars before she would buy the story" (189), since "How else was she to know the truth of what they said?" For Rufel, seeing is believing; to see is to know, a point providing an interesting challenge to contemporary feminist discourse that associates "looking," or the "gaze," with the masculine, dissociating it from the particularity of race. Rufel's eye objectifies and stabilizes the identity of the slaves at Sutton's Glen, a practice linked to her *racial* privilege.[23] References to slaves averting their gazes and lowering their lashes in her presence figure throughout Rufel's narrative (134, 139, 143).

For any distance to be bridged between Rufel and Dessa, Rufel must suspend the notion that only visual, empirical evidence can verify the truth of Dessa's abuse. Instead, she must rely on her imagination, the act not of objectifying but identifying with, of getting into another's place. As she listens to Nathan recount Dessa's story, Rufel "could almost feel the fire that must have lived in the wench's thighs," the "branding iron searing tender flesh" (138). She expresses disgust at "that vicious trader," "to violate a body so" (135). She asks sympathetically, "How did they bare such pain?" (138). Importantly, she uses the word "bare," again suggesting the visual, not "bear."

Significantly, Rufel hears the story not from Dessa herself, but from Nathan. Dessa has avoided this public exposure as fiercely as she has hidden her bodily scars. To expose them is to expose the horrors of victimization, to participate symbolically in a slave auction—to be publicly exhibited, displayed. Further, this "history writ about her privates" (21), is a script written in the slavemaster's hand and bound up in his enslaving psychosexual myths and fantasies. Here, Dessa's body is *her* text and, owning it, she has the right to disseminate it when and to whom she will. For Dessa, concealing the story from Rufel is just that—a radical act of ownership over her own body/text in a system that has successfully stripped slaves' control over their most intimate property. Because Dessa perceives Rufel's physical relationship with Nathan as the theft of a possession, it is no wonder that she wants to own her story.

Additionally, to publicize this "history writ about her privates"
is synonymous with baring a past too painful to bear.

III

> The future was a matter of keeping the past at bay.
>
> Toni Morrison
> *Beloved*

Dessa's refusal to confess the intimate details of her life to
either Nehemiah or Rufel is both an act of resistance (she is
the repository of her own story) and a means of containing her
pain by forgetting the past. Her refusal to "confess" to Nehemiah and Rufel is understandable, but Dessa is not more
able to speak about her past in the atmosphere of trust and
caring at Sutton's Glen among the escaped slaves:

> Even when the others spoke around the campfire, during
> the day of their freedom, about their trials under slavery,
> Dessa was silent. . . . That part of the past lay sealed in
> the scars between her thighs. (58–60)

But, like so many African American novels, *Dessa Rose* links
getting "beyond" slavery to remembering it, paradoxically
burying it and bearing it, a process exemplified in the naming
of Dessa's baby. Consistent with her desire to bury the past,
Dessa rejects Nathan's suggestion to name the baby after
Kaine, his father. "The baby's daddy, like that part of her life,
was dead; she would not rake it up each time she called her
son's name." And so she wants to name the baby after the men
who rescued her from Nehemiah. Rufel (again, possessed of
the power to "name") strikes a compromise by suggesting a
name that incorporates both tenses: "Desmond Kaine"—
"Des" for Odessa, "mond" to represent the men . . . who were

responsible for his free birth" (148), and "Kaine" to represent
the past.

The child is the evidence that forgetting the past cannot
be willed so easily. "Even buried under years of silence [she]
could not forget," but she chooses to undergo the process of
remembering in the presence of other slaves. When she does
begin to tell her story in her own voice, in the final section of
the novel, she tells it first and mainly to an audience of black
women—a dominant pattern in African American women's
fiction—which points to the delicate relationship between
teller and listener, writer and audience, in the establishment of
textual authority.

Although Dessa slowly develops trust for Rufel, it is and
can only be a partial trust:

> I'd catch myself about to tell . . . some little thing, like I
> would Carrie or Martha. . . . She did ask about that
> coffle and scraping out that cellar. I told her some things,
> how they chained us, the way peoples sang in the morn-
> ing at the farm. But I wouldn't talk about Kaine, about
> the loss of my peoples. . . . So we didn't talk too much
> that was personal. (216)

It should be noted here that Dessa does not share confidences
with Rufel, only details of a collective, historical record, details
in the public domain, if you will.

This is the difficult and precarious balance that contemporary novels about slavery must strike: between the public
record and private memory, between what Bakhtin calls "authoritative discourse" (privileged language, like sacred writ,
that permits no play with its framing context) and "internally-
persuasive discourse, . . . which is more akin to retelling a text
in one's own words."[24] Bakhtin's distinction coordinates with
the polarity between Nehemiah's and Dessa's discourse. The

novel plots the progressive movement away from Nehemiah's *written* "authoritative discourse," within which Dessa is framed (with all of the multiple valences of that term), and the emergence of Dessa's own story, *spoken* without Nehemiah's mediation in her own words and with her own inflections. To borrow from William Andrews, Dessa tells a "free story."[25]

Let me insert here that I do not mean to suggest, nor, I believe, does the novel, that because Dessa must *speak* text rather than *write* it, it is therefore *ipso facto* "freer" and without mediation—that because Dessa is illiterate, she is necessarily always self-present and thus has a higher claim to truth. Dessa's story is mediated largely by the operations of memory, but, by virtue of her social and material circumstances, her version of her story must be seen as more reliable than Nehemiah's could ever be. Moreover, in Dessa's section, the initial, sharply drawn distinction between orality and literary is complicated by recontextualization. Removed from the site of enslavement and oppression, the notion of "writing" is expanded and joined with speech. That complication is structured in Dessa's acquisition and use of the language of literacy, apparent in her repeated use of writing metaphors. Thinking back on her life with Kaine, Dessa expresses gladness that Kaine "wasn't Master, wasn't boss," adding "these wasn't peoples *in my book*" (184, my emphasis). Similarly, when she comes upon Nathan and Rufel making love, she fixes on the stark contrast between his blackness and the surrounding whiteness—"white sheets, white pillows, white bosom." "He wasn't nothing but a *mark* on them." From there, she generalizes about black-white relations: "That's what we was in white folks eyes, nothing but marks to be used, wiped out" (171). Though illiterate, Dessa understands the functional quality of language. She notices that, in organizing the flim-flam scheme, Harker, also illiterate, "made up some marks that wasn't writing but he used it like that" (195). Finally free to

wander about the town during one of the stops on the flim-
flam trail, Dessa indulges her fascination with the printer's
shop: "I couldn't see that printing machine often enough to
suit me," she says (215). And in a final gesture of valuation of
the written word, Dessa wants her story recorded, but importantly, she invests herself with the power and authority to validate it, for she has her son "say it back" (236) after he has
written it.

IV

Blow up the law, break up the "truth" with laughter.

Hélène Cixous
"The Laugh of the Medusa"

In the text that Dessa authorizes her son to tell, she
particularizes her experiences within more familiar generic
conventions of slavery. "I was spared much that others suffered" (176), she says—specifically, sexual abuse and sale on
the auction block. Unlike the familiar story of slavery, especially that told in antebellum slave narratives, the inflection of
laughter dominates Dessa's text, and I must add, it is not the
laughter fabricated in plantation myths of the happy darky
strumming on the old banjo. It is, rather, the laughter implied
in Cixous's "The Laugh of the Medusa"—"law-breaking"
laughter, "truth-breaking" laughter, or what Henri Bergson
describes in *Laughter* as "everything that comes under the
heading of 'topsyturvydom.' " According to Bergson, comedy
frequently sets before us a character ensnared in his own trap:
"the villain who is the victim of his own villainy, or the cheat
cheated." In every case, he concludes, "the root idea involves
an inversion of the roles, and a situation which recoils on the
head of its author."[26]

In Dessa's story, which is largely the account of a well-oiled scam, she and her comrades turn the "authoritative" text of slavery back on itself. They use all the recognizable signs of that text but strip them of their meaning and power. These escaped slaves contrive to sell themselves repeatedly back into slavery only to escape again. They exploit Southern law and custom and faithfully enact the narrow roles it assigns slaves and women. Dessa plays the "Mammy"; Rufel, the "Mistress"; and Nathan, her "Nigger driver." Allowing for the ever-present threat of discovery, they plan, if captured, for Dessa and the other slaves to "act dumb and scared," while Rufel is "to act high-handed and helpless" (194). In other words, they re-enter a familiar script and enact the roles it assigns, roles misread and misrecognized, which is classically demonstrated when Dessa is indeed recaptured by Nehemiah. He drags her to jail and alleges that she is an escaped slave matching the description on a reward poster: "Dark complexed. Spare built. Shows the whites of her eyes" (222). When the sheriff responds that the description "sound like about twenty negroes [he] knows of personally," Nehemiah orders Dessa to show her scars. From here Dessa has Southern gentility and patriarchy on her side. Both Nehemiah and the sheriff stand up when Rufel enters the room, who inveighs against scandalous people who "prey on defenseless womens" (226). Batting her eyes, she suggests that Nehemiah has simply mistaken Dessa for someone else, which gives Dessa confidence that the sheriff "couldn't take [his] word against the word of a respectable white lady," especially not in a dispute over something *down there*; "Cept for them scars, it was the word of a crazy white man against a respectable white lady" (226). In this system, Nehemiah's recourse is to *ask* Rufel if she would lie for Dessa. He *cannot* accuse her of lying, because a "white man ain't posed to call no white lady a lie" (227). The slave woman summoned to check Dessa's scars likewise denies that she has any. Ironically, then, the "evidence" the law uses to support its judgment to free Dessa comes not from Nehemiah, but from two women. More importantly, Dessa, who learned beforehand that "a nigger can't talk before the laws, not against no white man" (49), and who admitted at one time that she had "no idea what a 'court' was" (55), stands before the sheriff, the servant of the law, and Nehemiah, one of its archdefenders, and pleads her case. These women, all three victimized by Southern patriarchy and its racial and sexual politics, find a power within that system by turning it back on itself, by turning its assumptions about blacks and women topsy-turvy.

And except for that narrow escape, they have fun in the process, calling up "the comical things happened on the [flim-flam] trail" (216). As Dessa says,

> We laughed so we wouldn't cry; we was seeing ourselfs as we had been and seeing the thing that had made us. Only way we could defend ourselves was by making it into some hairraising story or a joke. (208)

She continues, "I told myself this was good, that it showed slavery didn't have no hold on us no more" (213).

V

Am I suggesting something as outlandish, to say nothing of its moral repugnance, as that Dessa's story would have us see that slavery was an institution to be laughed at, laughed about, laughed over? Clearly not. This is no book of "laughter and forgetting," to pinch from Milan Kundera, no dramatization of the thesis that slavery was not really "so bad" after all. It clearly was, and the historical record on that score is well known. For nearly four centuries, millions of human beings were kidnapped, some willingly sold into bondage by their own kin, and transported across the Atlantic to provide labor power that gave it the misnomer the "Peculiar Institution." But these all-too-well-known, horrific details were not the whole story, as historians such as John Blassingame, Eugene Genovese, Herbert Gutman, and Deborah Gray White have done well to establish.

Contemporary African American writers who tell a story of slavery are increasingly aiming for the same thing: to reposition the stress points of that story with a heavy accent on particular acts of agency within an oppressive and degrading system. In an interview that followed publication of *Beloved*, Toni Morrison explained that slavery was "so intricate, so immense and so long, and so unprecedented," that it can take the writer over. She adds, "We know what the story is. And it is predictable." The writer must, then, focus not on the institution but on the people, which puts the "authority back into the hands of the slave."[27]

To repeat, Dessa Rose is the final authority on her story, controlling her own text. But controlling a text of slavery, or any other text for that matter, especially a written one, is no guarantee of freedom. Triumph over language does not translate directly into triumph over social and material circumstances. The novel establishes this point most clearly after Dessa has escaped Nehemiah for the final time. Dessa and Rufel walk about the town of Arcopolis—an anagram of Acropolis?—with all the associations of logocentrism and law (polis), and yet what has developed between these two women is a threat to both the word and the law. They have threatened this system by challenging, if not escaping from, its terms. They free themselves from the mutual antagonism and distrust, the name-calling that assigns each a confining place and role. As they walk along, Dessa, now accustomed to calling

Rufel "Mis'ess," addresses her as such. Rufel answers, "I ain't your mistress. My name is Ruth." In a reciprocal gesture that reclaims her own "proper name," Dessa answers, "My name Dessa, Dessa Rose. Ain't no *O* to it" (232).

Dessa wants to hug Ruth at this point, but hugs her daughter instead. Throughout the novel their children have functioned both to mediate and mollify the differences between them and to symbolize the possibilities of a new order. We can say that *Dessa Rose*, and other contemporary novels of slavery, witnesses slavery after freedom in order to engrave that past on the memory of the present, but more importantly, on future generations that might otherwise succumb to the cultural amnesia that has begun to re-enslave us all and impoverish our imaginations.

6

Living in the Intersection of Womanism and Afrocentrism

Black Women Writers

Youtha C. Hardman-Cromwell

*I*n the mid-1800s Maria Stewart asserted her right as a black woman to be heard, writing:

> What if I am a woman: is not the God of ancient times the God of these modern days? Did he not raise up Deborah to be a mother and a judge in Israel? Did not Queen Esther save the lives of the Jews? And Mary Magdalene first declare the resurrection of Christ from the dead? . . . What if such women as are here described should rise among our sable race?[1]

Similarly, Anne Spencer wrote "Lady, Lady" prior to 1925, mocking Alfred Lord Tennyson's white masculine fantasy of an idealized womanhood. Spencer wrote:

Lady, Lady, I saw your hands,
Twisted, awry, like crumpled roots,
Bleached poor white in a sudsy tub
Wrinkled and drawn from your rub-a-dub.[2]

These women, both African American, wrote nearly a century apart, decades before Alice Walker coined the term *womanist* and long before Afrocentrism became a focus. Yet Spencer and Stewart gave expression to the sisterhood that binds black women writers together across the centuries. "They share the drive to define and redefine themselves in the past, present and future,"[3] refusing to be delineated by male and white models of femininity. In fact, Claudia Tate asserts that "by and large Black women writers . . . write for themselves as a means of maintaining emotional and intellectual clarity, of sustaining self-development and instruction."[4] Historically black women writers have claimed for black women the rights to self-esteem, self-determination, and celebration of their unique identity in a world inclined to treat blacks as nonpersons and black women as nonfemales.

If a womanist is one who views the world and makes decisions out of a consciousness of her identity as female and African American, and who values this identity, then black women writers began giving voice to womanism centuries before the term was employed. If an Afrocentrist is one whose lens for appropriating information and experiences is the unique worldview of Africa, and whose identity is partially rooted there, then African American women always have been living in the intersection of womanism and Afrocentrism, and their writers have given expression to this fact. The writings of black women are a significant source of evidence in support of this claim. In this chapter I argue that the terms *womanism* and *Afrocentrism* did not give expression to new ideas but named for us some values and self-definitions that had long been present in African American women's literature. Their poetry will be cited to support this assertion.

Afrocentrism in Black Women's Writing

Black women, including writers, have long sought the opportunity to live and write on their own terms with respect and dignity. Seeking to express the reality of black women's circumstances and dreams, the writers present "fascinating and complex women" who are "counterparts of black women in real life," according to Gloria Wade-Gayles,[5] but they also go beyond chronicling life. Tate notes:

> In fact, art seldom mimics life. An intermediary process involving reflection, distillation, organization, and most of all, imagination, separates the two realms. The writer projects her understanding of life, her vision as it were, into an imaginary world.[6]

Further, black women's literary contributions make use of the African heritage, which is central to the identity of the real women they make visible. As Katie Cannon observes:

> I have found that this literary tradition is the nexus between the real-lived texture of Black life and the oral-aural cultural values implicitly passed on and received from one generation to the next.[7]

She refers here to African storytelling, the oral history tradition. Toni Morrison has stated that she writes hoping that the sense of the storyteller is always in evidence.[8] This connection to African literary forms is also evident in the wordplay that is found so frequently in the work of the 1960s and that Sandi Russell identifies as part of the storyteller's art.[9]

Incorporation of these African elements can be seen in characters, settings, plots, and themes of black women's writing. Lorraine Hansberry's *A Raisin in the Sun*, for example, written in 1958, presents the theme of dignity as modeled in proud old black families through her portrait of Asagai, the Nigerian student.[10] The strong African concept of community, which sees personal identity primarily as communal, is reflected in the black woman's valuing of family and community and is mirrored in her literature. In an interview with Sandi Russell, Morrison called herself a "conduit for the tales of the tribe." Without realizing its import, Morrison chose for the name of the title character in the 1980 book *Sula* the word for "water" in the Tui dialect of the Ashanti language. In this book she tries to make the community, the neighborhood, "as strong a character as I could without actually making it 'The Town.' "[11] Morrison's concept of black community involves acceptance of difference, even differences that are not condoned. Everyone belongs. Speaking about *Tar Baby*, Morrison notes that "for me, the tar baby came to mean the black woman who can hold things together."[12] This symbolism is in harmony with the tar baby in African mythology.

Alice Walker reminds us:

> There is so much that is ours that we've lost and, we don't even know that we're missing it: ancient Egypt, ancient Ethiopia, Eatonville, Florida! And yet there's no general sense that the spirit can be amputated, that a part of the soul can be cut off because of ignorance of its past development.[13]

Thus Walker focuses her whole writing program on dealing with history, so that she will know where she is. She states:

> I can't move through time in any other way, since I have strong feelings about history and the need to bring it along. One of the scary things is how much of the past, especially our past, gets forgotten.[14]

This conviction is not new. Through the "Womanhood" section of *Annie Allen*, for example, published in 1942, Gwendolyn Brooks insists that "strong, secure, and independent black cultural bonds be established before Western culture can be savored."[15] As Earlene Stetson observes, "All the images that black women poets have created and explored over the centuries share this characteristic: they are more resonant because a specific historical heritage lies behind them."[16] She sees this heritage surface in the poets' use of imagery, citing Margaret Walker's *For My People*, written in 1942, to illustrate her point:

> For [Margaret] Walker, Africa is richly feminine — "sugar sands and Islands of Ferns" — as in Mississippi, with its "golden grain and purple fruit." Through this imagery and story, Walker recreates a collective black and female reality that is whole and yet separate from the mainstream of American ideology. It is this perception of a unified, unique reality that makes the poetry of black American women more than the simple outpouring of oppressed voices.[17]

We see African imagery used to give positive expression to this reality in Alice Walker's "Gift":

> *You intend no doubt*
> *to give me nothing,*

and are not aware
the gift has already been
received.
Curse me then
and take away
the spell.
For I am rich,
no cheap and ragged
beggar
but a queen,
to rouse the king
I need in you.[18]

Likewise, Gwendolyn Brooks included "Young Africans" in her 1970 collection, *Family Pictures*, and when Maya Angelou wrote in "For Us Who Dare Not Dare":

Taste one fruit
*   its juice free falling from a mother tree*
Know me
Africa.[19]

she gave voice to her feelings of connectedness to Africa in terms of her personal identity. Alice Walker expressed this same kind of African connectedness in the poems of Africa contained in her first published collection, *Once*. She had taken a vacation in Africa prior to the writing. In *The Color Purple*, too, she highlights the long historical links of black Americans with their African cousins through the letters between Celie in America and her sister Nettie in Africa, pointing out "that sexism is as prevalent in Africa as it is in America."[20]

Afrocentrism is a deliberate and conscious process of focusing upon our existence in terms of our African heritage and a reinterpretation of our identity and experiences in light of that heritage. In 1934, Zora Neale Hurston said:

While [the Negro] lives and moves in the midst of a
white civilization, everything he touches is re-interpreted
for his own use. He has modified the language, mode of
food preparation, practice of medicine, and most certainly the religion of his new country.[21]

Other writers consciously call the reader to envision and claim
the connection to Africa. Paule Marshall centers attention on the
Caribbean culture but continually uses "the theme of the black
woman's search for identity in a world bereft of ancestral connection."[22] Ntozake Shange chose her Zulu names as a protest
against her Western roots. Emphasizing "both the independence
and potential strength of the young black women for whom she
speaks," she chose *Ntozake* (she who comes with her own things)
and *shange* (she who walks like a lion).[23] Angelou was the author
of a television series on African traditions in American life,[24] and
Satiafa wrote in *For Dark Women*, published in 1982, a poem entitled "Rebirth," which begins, "I am a daughter of the Nile" and
contains in the third stanza these words:

> *Do not be deceived by false reports of your liberation.*
> *They would still steal or seal:*
> *The Heritage.*

The poem ends with these words:

> *Let all knowing and believing*
> *people who have endured*
> *Hear and rejoice in the rebirth*
> *Of our collective pride in our experience, and*
> *The Heritage.*[25]

The title piece of *For Dark Women* protests the low regard that
dark-skinned women must often endure. Satiafa wrote:

I always say: "You don't have to be beautiful to be clean."
"A little hiding helps a lot
When you got a shape like yours;
Looks like one of them
aff-rii-can women."

Countering such denigration, she continues in stanza two
with this summons:

Join with us.
Come, be proud, Ebony one.
You are rich with a beauty few have eyes to see . . .
In this place of mostly white folks, and
Old colored people, and
Left-over Negroes, and
Anglo Afro-Americans
Who
    Reject
    DARK women.

We call to you
Out sisters of deep tones
To walk with us,
Proud in your symbol of a noble past;
    Of Queen Mother and warrior women . . .
    Of mothers of the world race.
Stand tall, DARK woman. . . .[26]

Affirming Black Womanhood

Satiafa's words bring the issue of self-esteem to the forefront.
Raising self-esteem is one of the supporting bases for the
Afrocentric movement, but women found the Black Power
movement of the 1960s demanding a submissive posture from
black women. It elicited a powerful response from black

women writers. For example, Carolyn Rodgers wrote in "Poem for Some Black Women":

> *we live with fear.*
> *we are lonely,*
> *we are talented, dedicated, well-read*
> *BLACK, COMMITTED,*
>
> *we are lonely.*[27]

Her poem "I Have Been Hungry" expresses the challenge of knowing oneself:

> *The most beauty i am i am inside*
> *and so few deign to touch i*
> *am a forest of expectation.*
> *The beauty that i will be is*
> *yet to be defined.*
>
> *what i can be even i can not know.*[28]

Shange asserts that the reason she wrote *for colored girls* between 1972 and 1974 was so the "colored girls" could know what she had not known: the truth about what it is like to be a grown woman, not the myths and lies Shange had received from the mothers. She says:

> The mothers know that it's a dreadful proposition to give up one's life for one's family and one's mate and, therefore, lose oneself in the process of caring and tending for others. To send one's daughter off to that kind of self-sacrifice in silence with no preparation is a mortal sin to me. To do this without letting her know that this is a sacrifice is so unnecessary. To break this silence is my responsibility; and I'm absolutely committed to it. When I die, I will not be guilty of having left a generation of girls behind

thinking that anyone can tend to their emotional health other than themselves.[29]

So Shange wrote in *for colored girls:*

> . . . *cuz I don't know*
> *anymore/how to avoid my own*
> *face wet wit my*
> *tears/cuz i had convinced*
> *myself colored girls had no*
> *right to sorrow. . . .*[30]

And Alice Walker wrote in "Lost My Voice: Of Course./for Beanie":

Lost my voice?
Of course.

You said "Poems of
love and flowers are
a luxury the Revolution
cannot afford."

Here are the warm and
juicy vocal cords,

slithery,
from my throat.

Allow me to press them upon
your fingers,
as you have pressed
that bloody voice of yours
in places it could not know
to speak,
nor how to trust.[31]

Tate, summarizing this emphasis in the women's work, remarks, "What these writers are saying is that women must assume responsibility for strengthening their self-esteem by learning to love and appreciate themselves—in short, to celebrate their womanhood."[32] She notes that while the black heroine of black women's work is not "unconcerned about self-esteem and about attaining a meaningful social position," that "quest of self-discovery has different priorities and takes place in a different landscape."[33] These priorities reflect their concern for their children, their spouses, their families, their community; and the landscape of their quest is the black community, embracing its own culture and beliefs. Sandi Russell suggests that "the African-American writer realized that in order to be 'herself' in the present, she had to re-capture and re-define her past."[34] This attitude, in opposition to those formed during the period from 1940 to 1960, was expressed by a repudiation of the literature of American middle-class culture, its values, "and all the things—the good, on occasion, along with the bad—for which that culture stands."[35] It was institutionalized in such changes as the introduction of Black Studies programs in higher education, an effort joined by such black women writers as Sonia Sanchez. As a result, young people like Sandi Russell discovered a whole new aspect of themselves, changing the way they saw their history—and their worth.

By the late 1960s, African American women writers had begun, self-consciously, what Russell calls "the task of reclamation; the renaming and reclaiming of black women's history and selfhood."[36] Black women poets approach the task by addressing two questions, which Stetson articulates in this way: "How do we assert and maintain our identities in a world that prefers to believe we do not exist? How do we balance and contain our rage so that we can express both our warmth and love and our anger and pain?"[37]

Margaret Walker explains that her approach to these tasks is to make the main character of what she writes a black woman because, "I'm interested in the black woman and feel that the black woman's story has not been told, has not been dealt with adequately."[38] Tillie Olsen claims that black women writers, in general, use their talents to make the reader aware of what "harms, degrades, denies development, destroys; of how much is unrealized, unlived; instead of 'oppressed victims,' they tell of the ways of resistances, resiliences."[39] They use their heroines self-consciously to affirm black womanhood.[40] Poet Nikki Giovanni observes that black women are the only group that "derives its identity from itself. I think it's rather unconscious but we measure ourselves by ourselves, and I think that's a practice we can ill afford to lose."[41] Brooks supports this assertion in her 1972 autobiography, where she acknowledges the importance of identity and individualism to black women:

> Black women must remember . . . that [the black woman's] personhood precedes her femalehood; that sweet as sex may be, she cannot endlessly brood on Black Man's blonds, blues, and blunders. She is a person in the world—with wrongs to right, stupidities to outwit, *with* her man when possible, on her own when not. She will be there, like any other, once only. Therefore she must in the midst of tragedy and hatred and neglect, in the midst of her own efforts to purify, mightily enjoy the readily available: sunshine and pets and children and conversation and games and travel (tiny and large) and books and walks and chocolate cake.[42]

Alice Walker reflects that same spirit in these lines advocating independence and individualism: "Expect nothing. Live frugally on surprise. . . . Be nobody's darling. Be an outcast."[43]

But the approach has another side—the focus on community. By tackling the taboo of lesbianism in *The Color Purple*, for example, Walker affirms the importance of female friendship in the black community as a vehicle for both restoration and freedom.[44] And in their book *Common Differences*, Gloria Joseph and Jill Lewis observe that community consciousness is what distinguishes black and white in the women's movement:

> The Black woman has to develop her political struggles in keeping with her personal consciousness, while at the same time maintaining her ties with the Black community. Her role in the Black community is as central to her survival as is her personal political development in sexual areas.[45]

In fact, Gloria Wade-Gayles observes:

> Sexual gymnastics are neither the problem nor the solution, for black women are not searching for new ways of making love. The old ways work when one essential about their personhood is in place . . . recognition of the women's need to be appreciated and loved and respected, to be valued not for what they do, but for what they are as persons.[46]

Shange puts it this way:

> I feel that as an artist my job is to appreciate the differences among my women characters. . . . What I appreciate about the women whom I write about, the women whom I know, is how idiosyncratic they are. I take delight in the very peculiar or particular things that fascinate or terrify them. Also, I discovered that by putting them all together, there were some things they all are repelled by, and there are some things they all are attracted to. I only discovered this by having them have their special relationships to their dreams and their unconscious.[47]

Personal, Cultural, Universal

To say that these black women are feminists limits in a way not consonant with reality. As Joseph and Lewis note, "The important point is that the so-called feminine characteristics do not carry the same meaning and messages for Black women as they do for White women."[48] Their history, social position, and needs are not identical. Shange speaks of resenting "having to meet somebody else's standards or needs, or having to justify their reasons for living."[49] It is this type of reaction that gave rise to the need to claim our unique challenge to patriarchy by means of the term *womanism*. It is a positive reaction to the void created by the inadequate agendas of the women's movement and the Black Power movement, for the former confirmed its racism and the latter failed to consider the effects of sexism. Tate notes:

> By virtue of their race and gender, black women writers find themselves at two points of intersection: one where Western culture cuts across vestiges of African heritage, and one where male-female attitudes are either harmoniously parallel, subtly divergent, or in violent collision.[50]

Black women's criteria for analysis and evaluation develop "out of the various coping mechanisms related to the conditions of their own cultural circumstances."[51] Those cultural circumstances—political, social, and economic—manifest themselves in the common approaches of black women to the work of creating literature. Beverly Guy-Sheftall affirms what Wade-Gayles finds unique in the black woman writer, namely "her complex treatment of race and sex, which is a manifestation of her more sensitive understanding of black womanhood."[52] Womanism and Afrocentrism give expression to efforts of black women writers "to construct their identity within the confines of racism and patriarchy"[53] without being completely defined by the reality of that confinement. Wade-Gayles refutes the charge that their work is not universal because it focuses on womanness and blackness,[54] as if the work of white or male writers that leaves out the black woman's experience represents the universal.

Black women have persisted in writing about their experiences from their own point of view, denying neither their gender nor their African heritage, but giving expression to both of these aspects of their identity in their writings. Black women continue to lead and chronicle the search for a meaningful place in their communities without sacrificing their own identities. They might well resonate to the sentiment that Langston Hughes voiced in his "Notes on Commercial Theatre":

Someday somebody'll
Stand up and talk about me,
And write about me —
Black and beautiful —
And sing about me,
And put on plays about me!
I reckon it'll be
ME myself.

Yes, it'll be me.[55]

As black women writers respond to the invisibility of black women in a racist and sexist environment, they live and write in the intersection of what we now call womanism and Afrocentrism.

This is not a phenomenon exclusive to African American women privileged to be published and to have as their life's focus and livelihood the written expression of thoughts alien to ordinary women. We all live at that intersection. In March of 1985 I penned these words:

Queen Sheba's younger sisters,
Displaying less beauty,
Possessing less power,
Deprived of golden store
Still dream their dreams,
Search their searches,
Reach their star-reaches,
Grasping for
Hope's fruition,
Faith's affirmation.
Negating that feared truth
Of
Dreams-all-deferred,
The endless odyssey,
Star-dust turned to ashes.

7

Black Women in Biblical Perspective

Resistance, Affirmation, and Empowerment

◆◆◆◆◆◆◆◆◆◆◆◆◆◆◆◆◆◆◆◆◆◆◆◆◆◆◆◆◆◆◆◆◆◆

Cheryl J. Sanders

Black Women's Biblical Encounters

The African American woman's encounter with the Bible begins during the era of slavery in colonial America. Phillis Wheatley (1753–1784), the first published African American woman poet, had been captured in Senegal, enslaved and educated in New England, and subsequently migrated to England. Her poem "The Black Beauty" alludes to the black woman portrayed in the Song of Solomon:

> *Black I am, oh! daughters fair!*
> *But my beauty is most rare.*
> *Black, indeed, appears my skin,*
> *Beauteous, comely, all within.*[1]

Maria Stewart (1803–1911), the first American woman of any race to give a public address, incorporated many biblical texts and expressions into her political speeches advocating women's rights and the abolition of slavery. She gives a brief but compelling summary of the biblical basis for women's empowerment to speak in her 1833 "Farewell Address to Her Friends in the City of Boston":

> What if I am a woman; is not the God of ancient times the God of these modern days? Did he not raise up Deborah, to be a mother and a judge in Israel [Judges 4:4]? Did not queen Esther save the lives of the Jews? And Mary Magdalene first declare the resurrection of Christ from the dead? Come, said the woman of Samaria, and see a man that hath told me all things that ever I did, is not this the Christ? St. Paul declared that it was a shame for a woman to speak in public, yet our great High Priest and Advocate did not condemn the woman for a more notorious offence than this; neither will he condemn this worthless worm. The bruised reed he will not break and the smoking flax he will not quench, till he send forth judgment unto victory. Did St. Paul but know of our wrongs and deprivations, I presume he would make no objections to our pleading in public for our rights. Again; holy women ministered unto Christ and the apostles; and women of refinement in all ages, more or less, have had a voice in moral, religious and political subjects. Again; why the Almighty hath imparted unto me the power of speaking thus, I cannot tell.[2]

Both Sojourner Truth and Harriet Tubman, perhaps the best-known African American women leaders in the struggle against slavery, were certainly biblically informed, if not biblically literate, as evidenced by their speeches and biographies. Generally, in the slave community both male and female religious leaders achieved positions of influence and respect on the basis of their strong faith, knowledge of the Bible and true Christianity, demonstrated commitment to the welfare of the slave community, and their ability to preach.[3]

For a population of Christians who were for the most part illiterate, biblical knowledge was acquired and transmitted primarily through songs, hymns, sermons, and testimonies. The value of the Bible to the slave community persisted despite the concerted efforts by white slaveholders, preachers, and missionaries to restrict biblical preaching and teaching among slaves to those texts which admonished submission and obedience. In his book *Jesus and the Disinherited*, Howard Thurman tells why his grandmother, a former slave, would not allow him to read to her from the writings of Paul, except for 1 Corinthians 13, the chapter on love:

> "During the days of slavery," she said, "the master's minister would occasionally hold services for the slaves. Old man McGhee was so mean that he would not let a Negro minister preach to his slaves. Always the white minister used as his text something from Paul. At least three or four times a year he used as a text: 'Slaves, be obedient to them that are your masters. . . , as unto Christ.' Then he would go on to show how it was God's will that we were slaves and how, if we were good and happy slaves, God would bless us. I promised my Maker that if I ever learned to read and if freedom ever came, I would not read that part of the Bible."[4]

Her critical approach to the Bible became a significant formative influence in Thurman's own thoughtful exegetical treatment of the meaning of the religion of Jesus for the oppressed.

Further evidence of the importance of the Bible to African American women is found in the memoirs and sermons of pioneering black female preachers and evangelists. Zilpha Elaw (b. 1790), Julia Foote (1823–1900), Jarena Lee (b.

1783), and Amanda Berry Smith (1837–1915) were preachers who left detailed autobiographies describing their evangelistic ministries.[5] In each case, the Bible is cited repeatedly as a key to understanding the events of their early lives, their experiences of conversion and sanctification, and their preaching. In particular, each woman adopts a specific scriptural text as a theme for her autobiography; indeed, the quotation of the Scriptures on the title page initiates a biblical emphasis that is carried out through the entire autobiographical text. Jarena Lee, the African Methodist Episcopal preacher who was endorsed by Bishop Richard Allen but never ordained, begins her autobiography with a quotation from Joel 2:28: "And it shall come to pass. . . . that I will pour out my Spirit upon all flesh; and you sons, and your daughters shall prophesy." Zilpha Elaw, an itinerant Methodist preacher who financed her own ministry along the Eastern seaboard, in the slave states, and in England, quotes 2 Cor. 3:5 on the title page of her autobiography: "Not that we are sufficient of ourselves to think any thing as of ourselves; but our sufficiency is of God." The title of Julia Foote's autobiography is taken from Zech. 3:2: "Is not this a brand plucked out of the fire?" Foote was a missionary, ordained deacon, and elder in the African Methodist Episcopal Zion Church. Amanda Berry Smith, widely regarded as one of the most powerful international evangelists of the nineteenth century, described how she prayed before writing her autobiography, and asked the Lord to give her "something from His Word that I may have as an anchor":

> Asking thus for light and guidance, I opened my Bible while in prayer, and my eye lighted on these words: "Now, therefore, perform the doing of it, and as there was a readiness to will, so there may be a performance also out of that which ye have." (2 Cor. 8:11)[6]

The study, interpretation, teaching, and preaching of the Bible formed the foundation of these women's ministries, which were successful in scope and impact, despite the opposition they encountered because of their race and gender. These women nevertheless exhibited a bold sense of African and female identity. When whites asked her if she would rather be white, Smith responded that "we who are the royal black are very well satisfied with [God's] gift to us in this substantial color. I, for one, praise Him for what He has given me, although at times it is very inconvenient."[7] Facing opposition to women preachers, Foote defends her right to preach with a carefully crafted overview and word study of pertinent New Testament texts:

> But the Bible puts an end to this strife when it says: "There is neither male nor female in Christ Jesus" [Gal. 3:28]. Philip had four daughters that prophesied, or preached. Paul called Priscilla, as well as Aquila, his "helper," or, as in the Greek, his "fellow-laborer." Rom. xv. 3; 2 Cor. viii. 23; Phil. ii. 5; 1 Thess. iii. 2. The same word, which, in our common translation, is now rendered a "servant of the church," in speaking of Phebe (Rom. xix. 1.), is rendered "minister" when applied to Tychicus. Eph. vi. 21. When Paul said, "Help those women who labor with me in the Gospel," he certainly meant that they did more than to pour out tea.[8]

Elaw, Foote, Lee, and Smith had to overcome many hardships and obstacles in order to respond faithfully to the call to preach. Moreover, it is obvious that the intended aim of each of these memoirs is to inspire the reader to seek a biblically based experience of conversion and sanctification.

Biblically Inspired Activism

Bible study can produce personal empowerment in the form of religious conversion or salvation, which is a direct consequence of confronting the claims and narratives of the Scriptures in light of one's own existence. Political empowerment comes as the converted individual matches responses and insights with others to undertake collective projects that implement the love ethic and justice imperatives of the Scriptures in dialogue and partnership with the community of Christian faith. The classic expression of biblically based political empowerment among African Americans is the black women's club movement, which has provided an independent forum for black women's leadership, activism, and ministry outside ecclesial structures since the late nineteenth century. In essence, it has been ecumenical, because leaders and rank-and-file members of the black women's clubs have generally been churchwomen for whom the clubs represent the opportunity to pursue political and social goals unencumbered by sexism, racism, and other factors that would normally impede black women's social progress and participation in political structures. The Bible has been a significant source of spiritual, ethical, and political empowerment for black women who have used social service clubs, educational institutions, and advocacy organizations as bases for social activism. It has supplied the chief rationale for their resistance to human suffering and oppression, mandated their moral teachings and practice, and resourced their affirmations of racial, cultural, and sexual identity. To illustrate briefly, the impact of the Bible as an inspirational influence can be discerned in the lives of three distinguished African American women activists of the twentieth century: Mary McLeod Bethune, Nannie Helen Burroughs, and Marian Wright Edelman.

Mary McLeod Bethune (1875–1955), founding president of Bethune-Cookman College and the leading black educator and activist of her time, embraced the gospel mandate with great seriousness throughout her career. She was the first African American to enroll in the Moody Bible Institute, where she received, according to her biographer C. G. Newsome, a "mighty baptism of the Holy Spirit. This experience, she confessed years later, made her effective in all that she thought, said, or did thereafter."[9] Nannie Helen Burroughs (1883–1961) launched the Woman's Convention, Auxiliary to the National Baptist Convention with her 1900 speech "How the Sisters Are Hindered from Helping." In 1909 Burroughs became the first president of the National Training School for Women and Girls in Washington, D.C., the "School of the 3 B's," which stood for Bible, bath, and broom. She saw these three elements—the study of the Bible, personal cleanliness, and a professional approach to domestic work—as tools for the advancement of black women in a racist and sexist society that afforded them severely limited opportunities for education and employment.[10] Burroughs wrote a booklet entitled *Roll Call of Bible Women*, which provides greatly embellished descriptions of 148 female biblical characters. The entry for the Candace, queen of Ethiopia, reveals what would be identified today as an Afrocentric feminist perspective on biblical interpretation:

> It seems that the Cushite nation believed in women's right. They knew how to obey, as well as to command; how to rule as well as to be ruled, when it related to their own dominion. Their queens were not embarrassed by their sex in the administration of their government; and their Ambassadors black and comely never failed to meet with due respect in the execution of their missions to Foreign Courts.[11]

More recently, Marian Wright Edelman, civil rights attorney and founder of the Children's Defense Fund, has referred to biblical faith in *The Measure of Our Success* (1992). Published as an open letter to her three sons, the book lists twenty-five lessons for life, the last of which, "Always remember that you are never alone," includes several references to her reading the Psalms at important rites and events in the life of her family.[12]

The Bible has continuing significance in the preaching of twentieth-century black women. Ella Pearson Mitchell has compiled three collections of black women's sermons: *Those Preachin' Women* (1985), *Those Preaching Women*, vol. 2 (1989), and *Women: To Preach or Not to Preach* (1991), which also includes sermons by black men. Virtually all of the thirty-nine sermons contained in the three books that were preached by black women ministers of various denominations are centered upon a biblical text, and each sermon presents creative readings and interpretations of what the Bible is saying to illumine contemporary concerns.[13] Black women's biblical preaching represents a significant arena for the intersection of womanist and Afrocentric approaches to the Scriptures, toward the end of using the spoken word to foster healing and wholeness in the black church and community.

Womanist Biblical Scholarship

In recent years there have emerged a number of articles and books representing the scholarly study of the Bible by black women who are professional theologians and exegetes. These writings have been heavily influenced by the development of historical-critical approaches to the Bible by white feminists such as Phyllis Trible and Elisabeth Schüssler Fiorenza.[14] The vantage point of the black female biblical scholars is also informed by the theology and biblical scholarship of black males such as James Cone and Charles Copher. They tend to rely upon black women's historical and literary sources in framing the modern experiential referents for biblical reflection. One of the first such efforts was "The Emergence of Black Feminist Consciousness," an article contributed by ethicist Katie G. Cannon to Letty Russell's 1985 anthology *Feminist Interpretation of the Bible*.[15] In the final paragraph, Cannon alludes briefly, but importantly, to womanist consciousness as an interpretive principle for black women's use of the Bible as a strategy for resisting oppression. This allusion is important because it signifies that the question of what the Bible means to black women engendered a document that has become the pioneering statement of the womanist perspective in religious studies. In 1988 Renita J. Weems published *Just a Sister Away*, a book of womanist reflections upon women's relationships in the Bible. Weems imaginatively reconstructs nine stories in light of the concerns and struggles of modern women. Her second book, *I Asked for Intimacy: Stories of Blessings, Betrayals, and Birthings* (1993), includes additional creative interpretations of biblical stories, but its main emphasis is Weems's own personal story.[16] Sheila Briggs, Katie Cannon, Clarice J. Martin, and Cheryl Townsend Gilkes joined forces to write articles dealing with the interdisciplinary approaches of African American biblical interpreters in *Semeia 47: Interpretation for Liberation* (1989).[17] Cain Hope Felder's edited anthology, *Stony the Road We Trod: African American Biblical Interpretation* (1991), features two substantive articles on black women's interpretations of the Bible: "The *Haustafeln* (Household Codes) in African American Biblical Interpretation: 'Free Slaves' and 'Subordinate Women' " by Martin and "Reading Her Way through the Struggle: African American Women and the Bible" by Weems.[18] Felder's own "The Bible, Black Women and Ministry," first published in the Fall 1984/Spring 1985 issue of the *Journal of the Interdenominational Theological*

Center, is an attempt to set forth biblical images and themes pertinent to the religious leadership of black women. Theologian Delores S. Williams has authored a book devoted to the theological interpretation of the biblical character Hagar in relation to womanist concerns, aptly titled *Sisters in the Wilderness* (1993).[19] *Helpmates, Harlots, and Heroes* (1994) by Alice Bellis, a white feminist biblical exegete, is a book of women's stories in the Hebrew Bible interpreted in dialogue with womanist perspectives and scholarship, and designed for use in religious education classes in churches and synagogues.[20]

Feminist biblical studies have provided much of the impetus toward the methodological reorientation to the study of the Scriptures being embraced by African American female biblical scholars. Afrocentric biblical studies are significant for modern African American women in all walks of life because of what they reveal about the history of African women's engagement with the divine. The contemporary vantage point of living in the intersection of black and female identity brings a peculiar dynamic to bear upon the reading and appropriation of biblical texts. The interpreter becomes attentive to: (1) resistance to evil by employment of bold or unusual strategies, (2) affirmation of the good in terms of identity, loyalty, and values, and (3) empowerment as the manifestation of divine and human intervention in the life situations of women of African descent. Interpretation in the intersection of race and sex is based upon two important assumptions, namely, that women are important subjects and protagonists in the biblical narratives, and that national identity and racial distinctiveness are self-consciously addressed in the Scriptures through these characters. In other words, it is imperative to challenge traditional assumptions held by white people and black men who may disregard sex or race as meaningful categories for the analysis of biblical texts, and to explore ways of applying such insights to the construction of a normative understanding of the relevance of the Scriptures to black women's struggles and triumphs. This approach will be illustrated here with reference to four African women in the Bible—Hagar, Zipporah, the Queen of Sheba, and the Queen of the Ethiopians.

Four African Women in the Bible

Hagar (Genesis 16:1–15; 21:8–20). Hagar's story is given more attention by the biblical writers than that of any other African woman. Her importance in the African American folk tradition is secured by the affirmation that "we are Aunt Hagar's children," an indication that from the time of slavery African Americans have identified with the plight and promise of Hagar as a woman exploited and disinherited by the oppressor, but blessed and empowered by God. She was an Egyptian slave who was forced by her infertile mistress Sarai to submit sexually to the patriarch Abram in the role of surrogate mother. Her name may mean "flight." She twice encounters God in the desert—first when she flees Sarai's abusive treatment while pregnant, and a second time after she and her son Ishmael have been sent away by their former slavemasters to fend for themselves or die. In the first case Hagar hears a divine mandate to return and submit to slavery; in the second the divine voice directs her to receive promise and provision on behalf of her son empowering them both to live. There is ample evidence of resistance to evil, the affirmation of good, and divine empowerment in Hagar's story when read from a black woman's point of view.

Given the legacy of slavery and the current plight of African American women who are single parents struggling against a host of economic and social forces that threaten to destroy them and their children, a modern reading of Hagar's story would focus attention upon her slave status, her distinctive racial identity, her sex, and her role as the single parent of a son who is predisposed toward violence ("he shall be a wild ass of a man, with his hand against everyone," Gen. 16:12a). It is not made clear in either text how Hagar came to be a slave to Sarai and Abram. However, it is safe to assume that her slave status was not a consequence of her race, because if anything the Egyptian would be considered socially and culturally superior to her slavemasters. Perhaps her employment as a handmaiden is analogous to the modern practice of affluent white Americans who hire college-educated European *au pairs* to care for their children. She is forced to play the role of surrogate mother, and this sexual exploitation reflects the disadvantaged position of the enslaved females in the history of American slavery, who were sexually abused as women and were deprived of all rights to their own children. In modern Western societies, surrogate motherhood is presented as an option mainly for affluent infertile white women, who employ sophisticated reproductive technologies to produce offspring who are genetically related to mother and/or father. Typically the surrogate mother is a woman of lower economic and social status. By contrast, Hagar's surrogacy is characteristic of the "low-tech," unsophisticated approach known from slavery times of forcing slave women against their will to submit sexually to white or black males to produce children who are regarded as the slaveowners' property. Like Sarah, many white slave mistresses abused their female slaves and held them in contempt on the basis of the illicit sexual relationships fostered by their own husbands. Hagar's initial resistance to the evil of sexual and psychological abuse is to run away. But the angel directs her to return, to submit herself again to slavery, presumably because it would be impossible for her to survive alone in the wilderness in her pregnant state. Hagar's story takes a peculiar turn when Sarah's infertility is miraculously reversed, and she bears a son of her own. Hagar is disowned and sent away with her son from the material security of slavery. Sarah's deeper motive is to ensure that Ishmael, Abraham's heir, will be disowned and disinherited when he and his mother are banished to the wilderness: "Cast out this slave woman with her son; for the son of this slave woman shall not inherit along with my son Isaac" (Gen. 21:10). Abraham is reluctant to do so because evidently he feels some compassion toward his slave son, as was the case with some white slave-masters who made provision for their slave offspring in terms of material needs and educational opportunity. But he is directed by God to submit to his wife's order to cast out the slave woman with her son, just as in the earlier text he "listened to the voice of Sarai" and "went in to Hagar." This scenario posits the patriarch Abraham as being in full submission to his wife, against his own will but in obedience to God. Notwithstanding the interpretation offered in 1 Peter 3:6a, "Thus Sarah obeyed Abraham and called him lord," and the admonition of some modern interpreters that the Bible dictates that the husband be the sole authority in the marriage relationship, it is clear that Abraham's patriarchal authority was forfeited in the matter of what to do with Hagar.

Hagar resists evil by running away in the first instance, and by weeping aloud in the wilderness in the second. Her acts of resistance are closely connected with her affirmations of the goodness of God, who intervenes on her behalf. The key to understanding this connection is the act of naming, which in turn is related to hearing and seeing as alternative ways of knowing and being known by God. When she runs away, she is encountered by God in the wilderness. The angel directs Hagar to name her unborn son "Ishmael," which means "God hears," specifically, that God has given heed to her affliction and suffering *as a slave*. Next, Hagar is empowered by being granted a divine promise of innumerable offspring analogous to what was promised to Abraham: "I will so greatly multiply your offspring that they cannot be counted for multitude" (Gen. 16:10). Then Hagar does a most remarkable thing, making a bold affirmation of the divine presence unparalleled in the Scriptures—she names God! "So she named the Lord who spoke to her, "You are El-Roi"; for she said, "Have I really seen God and remained alive after seeing him?" (Gen. 16:13). This is an authoritative act unmatched by any of the male patriarchs and prophets; even the lawgiver Moses must ask God's name, because he is not empowered to name God. The name Hagar chooses means "God sees." Thus, in the name given by the angel to her unborn son, and in the name given by Hagar to God, there is a harmony of hearing and seeing. In the first text, God hears Hagar and promises that she and her offspring can live on the condition that she return to bondage. Hagar sees, thus God is revealed as one who responds to the cries of the oppressed and gives them life. In the second text, God hears Ishmael, but speaks to Hagar from heaven:

> "What troubles you, Hagar? Do not be afraid; for God
> has heard the voice of the boy where he is. Come, lift up
> the boy and hold him fast with your hand, for I will make
> a great nation of him." (Gen. 21:17–18)

This text speaks powerfully to the black single parent, in several ways. The fact that God hears the boy but speaks to the mother suggests that God holds the parent accountable for knowing and voicing the plight of the child. God counsels this single mother not to be troubled or afraid, because God has heard the cries of her child "where he is," that is, in the context of the child's present suffering and jeopardized future. In contrast to Hagar's first encounter with God, where she is told to return to slavery, in this encounter she is directed to "lift up" her child, and "hold him fast with your hand," emboldened and reassured by the promise that God will make of him a great nation. Thus by God's word the mother's highest aspirations for her son are affirmed. Especially meaningful to modern black mothers is the awareness that Hagar experienced the glorious empowerment of having God open her eyes, enabling her to see the provision of life-giving water in the desert, in other words, so that she could envision her family's future. If there is a miraculous intervention here, it is not providing water in the desert, but rather it is the blessing of insight and awareness. It is God showing the mother that the very thing she needs for her family's survival is within her reach. The text declares that "God was with the boy, and he grew up" (Gen. 21:20). Hagar's strong parental involvement with her son leads her to get him an Egyptian wife, which can be seen as an act of affirmation of her African identity. Ishmael and Isaac are reunited at the death of their father, Abraham. "His sons Isaac and Ishmael buried him in the cave of Machpelah" (Gen. 25:9a). Both become the progenitors of twelve tribes (Gen. 25:12–16). And in a very interesting turn of events, Isaac settles at Beer-lahai-roi, the site of the well named by Hagar for the "God of seeing." The ultimate impact of the Egyptian mother's affirmation of African identity, loyalty, and values upon her son is subtly expressed in the passage describing Ishmael's death: "he breathed his last and died, and was gathered to his people" (Gen. 25:17b).

This process of hearing, seeing, and naming stands as a vital witness against the notion that women are without voice and significance in the biblical world. However, Christian interpreters have tended to disregard the theological significance of Hagar's suffering and redemption, giving attention solely to the patriarch Abraham and his wife Sarah as the human embodiment of the divine theme of promise and fulfillment. Hagar's importance has been memorialized by the Islamic community, as indicated by the ritual re-enactment of Hagar's flight to the wilderness by pilgrims at Mecca. Traditionally, Muslims understand themselves to be the descendants of Abraham, but as heirs of the promise through Hagar and Ishmael, instead of Sarah and Isaac. It is easy to overlook the fact that the promise and covenant given to Abraham are affirmed in the ritual of circumcision involving the patriarch and his son Ishmael; a unique bond seems to be established between father and son as they are circumcised at the same time. Moreover, it is only after the circumcision that Abraham and Sarah conceive Isaac. The story of Hagar and Ishmael is told to account for the centuries of hostilities in the Middle East between the Ishmaelites and the Israelites. But implicit in the biblical narrative is the suggestion that Hagar's son will avenge his mother's suffering by means of violence. What is evident, however, is that the roles of slave and slaveowner eventually are reversed for the Hebrews and Egyptians, beginning with the third generation of Abraham's progeny.

Hagar's story, as told in portions of chapters 16 and 21 of the book of Genesis, provokes an interesting comparison with the book's major slave narrative, the story of Joseph, comprising fourteen chapters (Genesis 37–50). Abraham's great-grandson Joseph is sold into slavery by his own jealous brothers, an act of spiteful response to Joseph's spiritual giftedness and his father Jacob's unwarranted favoritism. Joseph nonetheless rises to a place of prominence and authority in Egypt, and he assimilates Egyptian identity to the extent that his brothers do not recognize him as their Hebrew kin when they come begging for food many years later. Joseph is finally reunited with his father and brothers, but their journey to Egypt in pursuit of sustenance sets up the Exodus experience of bondage and liberation generations later.

The plight of the male Hebrew slave represents an alternative model of life after emancipation. Hagar resisted slavery initially by running away; Joseph resisted slavery by being promoted to power. The Egyptian female slave Hagar is emancipated, actually cast out, at the initiative of her cruel and abusive mistress Sarah, who overrules Abraham's apparent desire to maintain a relationship with the slave woman and their son. Hagar's fate requires her to exercise absolute trust in God, who makes provision for her in the wilderness and is an abiding presence and protection for her and her son. She and Ishmael do not remain isolated and marginalized, however; she ensures their ongoing relationship with their people through Ishmael's marriage to an Egyptian wife. Joseph also marries an Egyptian wife, but emancipation for him means assimilation of the values of the dominant culture, and acquisition of its power and wealth. Both are victims of sexual exploitation (Joseph being imprisoned because of being falsely charged with rape by his master Potiphar's wife after her botched effort to seduce him), both are emancipated from slavery, and both are divinely empowered to live as free persons with their families. But Joseph's ascension to power has double consequences for his kin; they are fed by the Egyptians in a time of famine, but after the death of Joseph the Egyptians enslave and oppress his people. On the other hand, Hagar's empowerment results in her son becoming a patriarch in his own right, whose descendants are destined to remain perpetually at war with their Hebrew cousins. Her story is an inspiration to black mothers living in a society that would deny them access to power and material provision for their children, but who seek to survive and thrive with their families on the basis of trust in a God who sees and hears and reveals divine power and provision in the very deserts of their despair. Joseph's story may be an inspiration to oppressed black males who would aspire to the highest positions of authority and resource management within the hierarchies of the dominant group on the basis of personal charisma and wit. Indeed Joseph was a devout and righteous man, and a faithful and

compassionate father, but the price he paid for personal afflu-
ence and success was strained relations with his own people and
deep identity conflicts on the basis of culture and nationality.

Zipporah (Exod. 2:21–22; 4:24–26; Num 12:1). Zipporah, a
Cushite (black) woman, was the daughter of Jethro, the wife
of Moses, and the mother of Gershom, whom she circumcised
during a crisis in the relationship between Moses and God.

As Moses returned to Egypt in order to show his divinely
ordained powers before the court of Pharaoh and to request
the release of his people from bondage, the text declares, "the
Lord met him and tried to kill him" (Exod. 4:24b). To save
her husband's life, Zipporah performs a bold and unusual act
of resistance—she circumcises her son, and touches Moses' apparently uncircumcised genitals with the son's bloody foreskin:

> But Zipporah took a flint and cut off her son's foreskin,
> and touched Moses' feet with it, and said "Truly you are
> a bridegroom of blood to me!" So he let him alone. It
> was then she said, "A bridegroom of blood by circum-
> cision." (Exod. 4:25–26)

Interestingly, this is not the first time Moses was rescued by an
African woman; while bathing in the Nile River the daughter
of Pharaoh had found the infant Moses floating in a basket
among the reeds, took pity on him, and adopted him as her
own son (Exod. 2:5–10). Perhaps the fact that he was raised
by an Egyptian accounts for Moses' uncircumcised state. In
any case, Zipporah clearly has disregarded social conventions
concerning a priestly ritual performed exclusively upon males
by males, but, after all, her own father was a priest. This symbolic act of circumcision not only protects Moses from death
but can also be seen as an important step in his initiation and
authorization to engage in the ministry of liberation. Zippo-

rah takes the initiative to resist the threat of death and to
affirm the required covenantal relationship on behalf of her
husband, who in turn is divinely empowered as a consequence
of her actions.

The reference to Moses' wife found in the book of Numbers suggests that Miriam and Aaron's criticism of Moses'
marriage to a Cushite woman is grounded in sibling jealousy
and resentment. It may be that the underlying issue is who is
invested with the charismatic authority to speak for God,
rather than the appropriateness of interracial or cross-cultural
marriage per se. After the Lord speaks an angry word of
rebuke against both Miriam and Aaron for challenging Moses'
prophetic status, she is singled out for punishment. Ironically,
her punishment for criticizing Moses' marriage to the black
woman is to become, at least temporarily, "as white as snow."

Queen of Sheba (1 Kings 10:1–13; 2 Chron. 9:1–9). The
Queen of Sheba was an Ethiopian monarch who tested Solomon's wisdom with hard questions, blessed him, and traded
with him. She represents one of two types of female monarchs
found in the Bible, those who are reigning monarchs in their
own right and those whose authority is derived from, and limited in relation to, their husbands. It would seem that African
women alone achieved status as monarchs in an otherwise patriarchal biblical world. Against the typical assumption made
by many readers and interpreters that women in the Bible have
no voice, authority, or importance in comparison to men, it is
evident that this African queen was not only head of state but
also Solomon's diplomatic peer. Moreover, she arrives in
Jerusalem with an impressive entourage, taking the initiative
to match wits with a king whose wisdom and wealth had been
divinely bestowed. Her visit to Jerusalem can be understood as
an act of resistance, in the sense that she felt compelled to
verify the rumors she had heard in her own land concerning

the greatness of Solomon. She has resisted the pitfall of misinformation! Given the intellectual and political greatness of Solomon, it is certainly significant that Solomon is tested and endorsed by an African woman. So impressed is the queen by his wisdom and prosperity that she offers a blessing affirming Solomon's God and his royal imperative to rule with justice and righteousness:

> Blessed be the Lord your God, who has delighted in you and set you on the throne of Israel! Because the Lord loved Israel forever, he has made you king to execute justice and righteousness. Then she gave the king one hundred twenty talents of gold, a great quantity of spices, and precious stones; never again did spices come in such quantity as that which the queen of Sheba gave to King Solomon. (1 Kings 10:9–10)

Conveyance of expensive gifts in such great quantities to a wealthy foreign monarch demonstrates the African queen's material empowerment to accumulate and distribute wealth. Jesus recalls the investigative mission of the Queen of Sheba in his prophetic discourse with the scribes and Pharisees:

> The queen of the South will rise up at the judgment with this generation and condemn it, because she came from the ends of the earth to listen to the wisdom of Solomon, and see, something greater than Solomon is here! (Matt. 12:42; Luke 11:31).

Thus Jesus prophesies the resurrection of this Queen of Sheba to condemn those who ask for a sign from Jesus but disregard the significance of his teaching and his works. His statement somewhat prefigures the symbolic importance of the Ethiopian Queen who authorizes her emissary to worship in Jerusalem and bring the Christian gospel home to Africa.

The Candace, Queen of the Ethiopians (Acts 8:27). The only explicit reference to an African woman found in the New Testament is the Candace, the Ethiopian or Nubian monarch whose treasurer was converted by Philip. She is actually only mentioned in passing; the main subject of the text is the treasurer himself: "Now there was an Ethiopian eunuch, a court official of the Candace, queen of the Ethiopians, in charge of her entire treasury. He had come to Jerusalem to worship and was returning home" (Acts 8:27b). "Candace" is the queen's official title. Although the biblical text gives little detail about the Candace, she is portrayed as yet another African queen who is a reigning monarch in her own right. It is apparent that the New Testament attests to the Old Testament pattern of female authority and power in Africa. The stories of these two queens invite further comparisons. The Queen of Sheba journeyed to Jerusalem in person to investigate King Solomon; the Candace sends her emissary to worship in Jerusalem. The Queen of Sheba seeks to verify rumors and information about Solomon's reign; the Candace may have sent her emissary to gather information about religious developments in the city of Jerusalem. On this view, it can be discerned that the Candace plays an important, if indirect, role in fostering the spread of the gospel to the Gentile world. The Ethiopian eunuch has been dispatched to Jerusalem to seek divine truth, and in the end he brings the gospel to Africa. Thus the initiative to present the gospel to the Gentiles can be credited to an African woman and her male servant, and not to Peter, Paul, or any of the Jewish male disciples of Jesus. Moreover, the fact that the first Gentile convert to Christianity is an African man usually gets overlooked by those who habitually disregard significations of race and culture in biblical texts, despite the fact that the Ethiopian's conversion occurs prior to the conversion of Saul, the persecutor of Christians, or of Cornelius, the Roman military officer.

The major theme of this discussion has been the view of the Bible as divine documentation of black women's historic encounters with God, which today begs for further study, attention, promotion, especially by those with a concern for the survival and empowerment of black women. This is not merely an interpretive scheme devised to promote black women's self-esteem. Rather, it is an attempt to uncover the truth, to review the record in the light of current experience and illumination, that God has dealt with black women in ancient times and is yet speaking to black women today. The issue of women's leadership in the family, church, and society is of critical concern here, because of the tendency of some to devalue the leadership of women on the ground of the Scriptures. Upon closer scrutiny of its accounts of black women's lives, the Scriptures reveal God's sustenance of the single mother, the faithful wife, the devout poor, and the virtuous privileged. In particular, it is Hagar's story that speaks most directly to today's black woman, not just because of the common ground of black female identity, but also because her story shows that the class of people now despised in church and society were not devalued and disregarded by the God of the biblical world. On the contrary, women are key players in salvation history, including the enslaved woman. Abraham, Moses, and Solomon, three of the greatest men in the history of Israel, formed intimate (though sometimes exploitative) relationships with African women, and they all experienced divine promise and blessing in the context of these partnerships.

In view of the stories of these biblical African women, it can be concluded that with God there is always the possibility of choices, alternatives, or escape. Oppression has been defined as the absence of choices, but in biblical perspective God always enables people to choose, to exercise freedom, and to resist evil in the form of oppression and the threat of death.

However, it is also necessary to face the consequences of wrong choices, yet with the possibility of repentance and forgiveness. This, of course, is the good news of the gospel of Jesus Christ, that we can choose better, we can do better, whatever our race, sex, or station in life, by resisting evil and affirming what is good in ways that empower our neighbors as well as ourselves.

PART ◇ THREE
LEARNING

8

Teaching Womanist Theology

◆◆◆◆◆◆◆◆◆◆◆◆◆◆◆◆◆◆◆◆◆◆◆◆◆◆◆◆◆◆◆◆◆◆

Kelly Brown Douglas

*T*wo years ago I anxiously prepared to teach, for the first time, womanist theology. Since my own theological training never provided me with an opportunity to do course work involving serious reflection on black women's experience, I was therefore excited to be able to offer students a chance to study theology that emerged from the lives and struggles of black women. Yet, when I sat down to develop the course, the gaps in my theological training conspired against me. I did not have a model for developing a course such as womanist theology. I did not know how to begin to teach students about black women's reality and theological concerns. I wrestled with how to structure the course so that it would do justice, in a fourteen-week semester, to the stories of those who had long been invisible in the theological academy.

The pedagogy I initially adopted had great potential for failure. It promised to kill any enthusiasm the students might have brought to the class. As I planned the course I relied on what I knew best and drew on the ways in which I myself had been taught. I opted for a lecture format, structured around particular theological themes. Students would read the assigned texts, and I would provide weekly lectures covering what I deemed the important issues. For instance, one week the students might read material focused around black women's understandings of God. I would then lecture on this same theme.

I had unwittingly designed "Womanist Theology" as a perfect example of "banking" education.[1] Banking education makes at least three assumptions. First, it assumes that students are empty vessels, banks ready to be filled. It does not value the student's experience or wisdom. Second, the banking system promotes one-directional communication. Only the teacher is considered capable of making deposits of knowledge. There is no appreciation for the possibility of teachers and students entering into dialogue as mutual learners. Finally, the banking model does not invite the students to interact with the course material. Critical examination of ideas and issues is not encouraged.

Fortunately, those who entered this course were not passive learners. They refused to be constrained by a fixed banking structure. They made clear that "what they should learn" was not going to be rigidly decided for them in advance. Each week they walked into the classroom discussing the reading material. Before I could start my lecture they were engaged in a lively conversation. They shared with each other what it meant finally to encounter the story of black women. Each student revealed the impact that this story had on her or his life. They were not passive receptacles of static facts but critical learners allowing themselves to be challenged by the reality of black women's struggles. This was confirmed when one black woman confessed, "I used to think what happened to me was personal; now I see it is just a part of being black and female." Within three class sessions, "Womanist Theology" was transformed from a banking format to one that was dialogical and interactive. In the process I was educated on how to teach such a course. I learned certain "musts" for teaching about those who have been "marginalized" in church, society, and academy, especially to those who suffer from that same marginalization.

I recognized that the students had actually changed the course into one more compatible with the womanist concept. The term *womanist* has now become a symbol for black women's experience. It points to the unique richness and complexity of black women's lives as they continually struggle to maintain life and to make it better for themselves and their families. In religious scholarship *womanist* signals an understanding of God, Christ, the Bible, and the church from the perspective of this particular struggle.

Although the meaning of the term now goes beyond Alice Walker's original definition of it, certain aspects of the definition are consistently highlighted by black female religious scholars.[2] These aspects seem also to suggest a womanist pedagogy.

Essentials of a Womanist Pedagogy

Dialogical: "Mama, I'm walking to Canada and I'm taking you and a bunch of other slaves with me."
"It wouldn't be the first time."

One of the attractive features of Alice Walker's definition is an intergenerational dialogue between a mother and daughter. A young girl tells her mother about her plan to gain freedom, and her mother then informs the girl that she would not be the first one to carry out such a plan. She provides her with an opportunity to learn from and become empowered by the freedom struggles of her foremothers. This dialogue suggests three essentials for womanist pedagogy: it must provide students with an opportunity to dialogue with black women's history, with "ordinary" black women, and with each other.

A course in womanist theology must provide students with an opportunity to encounter black women's history. This historical dialogue is especially important for black female students. It is through this dialogue that they can discover that their own experience of struggle is not simply personal, it is reflective of a wider historical experience. By becoming connected to their past, black female students can become empowered by the knowledge that they are not alone in their struggle for freedom. They are a part of a long history of black women trying to make do and do better. In general, through a historical dialogue, black female students can discern "when and where" they enter the story of black women struggling to nurture survival and freedom for themselves and their families.

The historical dialogue can also provide black female students with *role models*. They can learn from the stories of other black women. For instance, knowledge of black women's history provides them with an opportunity to encounter black women's "culture of resistance." This is a culture which, according to Patricia Hill Collins, black women have crafted to help them resist the dehumanizing and oppressive situations which they were forced to encounter.[3] This culture of resistance can serve as a guide to black female students as they negotiate their own reality of black womanhood.

Dialogue with black women's history is also imperative for students who are not black and female. It gives them a chance to discover their relationship to black women's history.

They can discern and confront the "history of relationship" between them and black women. An understanding of this relational history is important if there is to be any solidarity in the struggle for freedom. Such solidarity can occur only when the history which divides is honestly dealt with, and the history which connects is recognized.

As important as the historical dialogue is, an even more significant dialogue awaits. If womanist theology emerges from the experiences of black women in struggle, then conversation with these women is critical. The thought, experiences, and wisdom of these women must be the basis for womanist thought. Students of womanist theology, therefore, must be informed not simply by books but also by the ordinary women who are engaged in the day-to-day fight for survival and freedom. This means that a womanist theology class must go beyond the walls of the academy to the places where black women are actively resisting oppression of their families and community, that is, to the churches, community centers, and other local agencies and organizations.

Finally, in a womanist theology course students must dialogue with each other. An atmosphere and occasion must be provided for the students to talk to one another. To confront honestly their "history of relationships" they have to share how that history shapes who they are and how they now relate to each other.

> *Diversity of Experience*: "Mama, why are we brown, pink, and yellow, and our cousins are white, beige, and black?" *Answer:* "Well you know the colored race is just like a flower garden, with every color flower represented."

Throughout Walker's definition of the womanist concept there are various references to the diversity of the black community in general, and of black women in particular. A course compatible with the womanist concept should portray the richness and variety of black women's experience. For instance, the course should attempt to reflect black women's different economic situations, lifestyles, and ways of loving.

Exploring this diversity is beneficial for several reasons. First, it challenges the notion that all black women are alike. Such a narrow perception typically leads easily to stereotyping and allows one to avoid the varied challenges that emerge from a more comprehensive look at black women's lives.

Second, an introduction to the diversity of black women's experience prevents students from reading one black woman's story as if it were the whole story. It dispels any beliefs that if they have read one biography, narrative, or novel by a black woman then they have it all. To make students aware of the richness of black women's reality might motivate them to pursue further study of black women's history and culture.

Finally, exploration of black women's diverse experience provides an occasion for black female students to celebrate their own unique expressions of black womanhood. It may even help them to understand each other's uniqueness "as a dynamic human force which is enriching rather than threatening to [their own] defined self."[4] This becomes particularly crucial to helping black women refrain from marginalizing each other because of difference. For instance, one of the most divisive and explosive issues in courses which I have taught has been sexuality. Students have often been most strident in their antagonism toward gay and lesbian people. This is, in part, due to fear of and lack of respect for difference. It therefore becomes essential for students to confront their fears and biases by learning about and appreciating black women's rich differences. At the same time it becomes important for students to discover how their sense of "privilege" lends itself to the discrimination of others. This can also be done by exploring a womanist vision for freedom.

An Analysis of Oppression: "Committed to survival and wholeness of entire people, male and female."

Walker's definition points to a womanist's vision for freedom. This envisions a world where all persons, men and women, are at least respected and treated equally. A course that takes seriously this womanist vision must engage an analysis of black women's oppression. It must help students to name the social, economic, political, religious, and cultural barriers to black people's freedom. It must also compel students to recognize their own points of privilege and how they are themselves complicit in black oppression. They must begin to name the ways in which they benefit from as well as perpetuate racist, sexist, classist, and heterosexist structures.

What Does All This Have to Do with Theology?

The major underlying assumption of womanist theology is that it, like all theology, is fundamentally shaped by the social and historical experience of the persons doing it. This means that to appreciate fully what womanist theologians say about the meaning of God, Christ, the Bible, and the church, students must attain a basic knowledge of black women's experience. Only after gaining some familiarity with what it means to be black and female can students critically reflect upon black women's theological concerns and affirmations.

How has my pedagogy changed as a result of my first experience with teaching womanist theology? What am I doing two years later in my second attempt at teaching womanist theology? Most significantly, I have designed the course as a seminar. Practically, this means that the students are seated in a circle so that they can more easily talk to one another.

Second, during the introductory class session much of the time is spent with students telling each other "who they are" and why they have decided to take womanist theology. This is done to promote an atmosphere where students feel more comfortable entering into honest dialogue with each other. Third, discussion, not a lecture, is the central focus of the class. The students' critical responses and reactions to the reading shape the discussion. As the instructor, I attempt to facilitate their discussion and to sum up the salient issues raised by reading as well as by the students. Fourth and perhaps more importantly, field trips are planned so that the students can encounter and dialogue with black women outside of the academy who are actively engaged in moving the black community toward wholeness.

Remaining Challenges for Teaching Womanist Theology

The discussion thus far has been restricted to teaching womanist theology in the academy. As has been implied in this discussion, however, it is inappropriate for womanist theology to be restricted to institutions of higher learning. It does not emerge from there. It emerges from the life, wisdom, and faith of black women struggling for the well-being of their families and themselves. What Patricia Hill Collins calls "Black women's everyday, taken-for-granted knowledge" must be the foundation out of which womanist thought emerges. That is why it is imperative for students of womanist theology to engage black women beyond academic institutions. As Collins goes on to explain, it is this "taken-for-granted knowledge" that womanist scholars should rearticulate in such a way that it "empowers African-American women and stimulates resistance."[5] Herein lies the challenge for the teaching of womanist theology. Teaching womanist theology cannot be confined to colleges, universities, and seminaries. Womanist theologians must move beyond the academy. We must make this theology available to black church and community women. This is crucial for at least two reasons. First, if the wisdom which is gained from black women in struggle is to empower these very women, then it must be accessible to them. Second, womanist theology must be held accountable to black women in struggle. What womanist theology says about God, Christ, and the church must make sense, must ring true, to these women in the context of their daily struggles. The challenge therefore remains for womanist theologians to develop appropriate pedagogies for teaching church and community women. These pedagogies must not only be compatible with the womanist concept, but also grow out of the various contexts in which it is taught. The way in which it is taught in the seminary might not be appropriate for teaching church and community women. As I learned from my first experience of teaching womanist theology in the seminary, I expect to learn from church and community women as I move to make womanist theology more accessible to them.

I have no doubt that the more I teach womanist theology the more I will learn about how to teach it. I anticipate new challenges and new discoveries, even as I learn more about the womanist experience. Indeed, the most important and enduring essential for womanist pedagogy is flexibility. A womanist pedagogy must allow for change so as to embrace the complex and dynamic reality of black womanhood.

9

Afrocentric and Womanist Approaches to Theological Education

◆◆◆◆◆◆◆◆◆◆◆◆◆◆◆◆◆◆◆◆◆◆◆◆◆◆◆◆◆

Cheryl J. Sanders

I will begin by lifting up some of the methodological concerns connected with the Afrocentric and womanist ideas as modes of validating knowledge, norms, and experience. Then I will turn my attention to how these considerations illumine a path toward producing or enhancing Afrocentric and womanist pedagogies employed in theological education. Finally, I will consider some specific implications of the Afrocentric and womanist approaches for black theological education.

Bearings

The Afrocentric idea is rooted in the worldview and collective experience of the people of Africa and the African diaspora. Its central concern is to advance the position of African people in the world by affirming their identity and contributions and by unmasking the biases and limits of Eurocentrism. Afrocentric scholarship seeks to: (1) celebrate the achievements of African people and cultures; (2) analyze critically the hegemony of the Eurocentric worldview and ways of knowing that have served the interests of racial oppression, especially as they have skewed the self-understanding of African American educators and leaders; and (3) construct an alternative framework for understanding and evaluating human experience. The ultimate end of the celebrative, critical, and constructive dimensions of the Afrocentric impulse is, in the words of Afrocentrist Molefi Asante, to "move to harmony through rhythms that are the African path to transcendence."[1]

The womanist nomenclature has its origins in the thought of Alice Walker, who defined the term extensively in her 1983 collection of prose writings, *In Search of Our Mothers' Gardens.*[2] In essence, womanist means black feminist. As early as 1985, black women scholars in religion began publishing books and articles that employed the womanist perspective as a point of departure for doing theology, biblical studies, and ethics. These scholars include Jacquelyn Grant, Delores S. Williams, Kelly Brown Douglas, Renita Weems, Katie G. Cannon, and Toinette Eugene. The major sources for their work are the narratives, autobiographies, novels, poetry, prayers, and other writings that convey black women's traditions, culture, and history. The method developed to appropriate these sources can also be summarized in terms of its celebrative, critical, and constructive intent, inclusive of (1) the celebration of black women's historical struggles and strengths; (2) the critique of various manifestations of black women's oppression in terms of race, sex, and class; and (3) the construction of black women's distinctive theological and ethical claims toward a liberative praxis.

The Afrocentric idea as fully developed in the writings of Asante, and the womanist idea as defined in much briefer form by Walker, seem to bear more similarities than differences as epistemological statements. The following excerpt from the book *The Afrocentric Idea* strongly echoes the self-affirming and self-assertive aspects of womanism as an ethos of struggle and commitment to human survival and wholeness, culturally and historically grounded in the resistant posture of the slave:

> A truly Afrocentric rhetoric must oppose the negation in Western culture; it is combative, antagonistic, and wholly committed to the propagation of a more humanistic vision of the world. Its foundation is necessarily the slave narrative. Its rhythms are harmonious, discordant only to those who have refused to accept either the truth of themselves or the possibility of other frames of reference.[3]

The self-affirmation and self-assertiveness of womanism and Afrocentrism ought not to be regarded in individualistic terms, but rather should be understood as indicative of the self finding expression in harmony with others. This understanding is conveyed by the notion of love in the womanist definition, and as the *sudic* ideal in Afrocentrism. By coining the term *womanist* Walker is exercising the authority "to name ourselves after our own fashion."[4] Similarly, Asante emphasizes "the presence of *nommo* in African discourse and in specific instances of resistance to the dominant ideology," defining *nommo* as the generative and productive power of the spoken word.[5] The ultimate aim or end of self-actualization in the strongly collective sense is envisioned by the womanist as survival and wholeness of entire people, and as harmony and transcendence by the Afrocentrist. Although Asante clearly rejects Christianity as a valid religious option for Afrocentric people, he refers repeatedly to the black church experience to illustrate

Afrocentric values, spirituality, and culture. By contrast, Walker asserts that the womanist "loves the Spirit" without making reference to any specific religion. In both cases, black spirituality is acknowledged as a path to transcendence apart from any validation of black Christian identity.

The Witnessing Spirit, History, and Transformation

The problem of the validation of knowledge, norms, and experience within the African American context is a major concern for both womanist and Afrocentric scholars. I would propose a simple framework for analyzing the validation of womanist or Afrocentric claims based upon the concept of the "witness of the Spirit," a term drawn directly from the black church tradition, which I would augment to include two other criteria, the witness of history and the witness of transformation. By the witness of the Spirit I mean the collective "Amen" of assent, endorsement, or approval that is given by the people when a word or other personal expression is accepted as truth-bearing. The witness of the Spirit finds explicit expression in Asante's work as a criterion for the validation of Afrocentric discourse; "Harmony has been achieved when the audience says a collective 'amen' to a discourse, either through vocal or symbolic acknowledgment."[6] If we understand the witness of the Spirit as a spiritual transaction or communication always mediated by persons in some form of community, including family, then the intergenerational dialogue between mothers and daughters that undergirds the womanist definition can be interpreted as expressive of the witness of the Spirit as well.

The witness of history, with specific reference to the collective stories and traditions of African American people, is a significant mode of validation for both Asante and Walker. The historic struggle of black women against slavery and oppression is an intrinsic and foundational element of the womanist idea. History emerges as the single most important criterion for validation of Afrocentric knowledge, as indicated in Asante's critique of African American Christianity and Islam:

> He or she (the Afrocentrist) studies every thought, action, behavior, and value, and if it cannot be found in our culture or in our history, it is dispensed with quickly. This is not done because we have something against someone else's culture; it is just not ours. We do not have too many complaints with the person who decides to accept someone else's culture, religion or ideology, be it Islam, Christianity, or Marxism, if it serves him better than his own. However, for us it is impossible to see how anything from outside ourselves can compare with what is in our history.[7]

The witness of transformation emerges as a major criterion for validation in both womanist and Afrocentric thought. Here the notion of transformation is not to be interpreted in reductionist terms, but rather as an appeal to the power of the paradigm in question to bring forth change when applied to people's individual and collective lives under conditions of oppression. Walker cites such terms as "capable" and "in charge" to indicate the constructive criterion of the womanist ideal. In her statement of the womanist's commitment to survival and wholeness of entire people, and her portrayal of the womanist slave leading her people out of bondage, Walker illustrates some of the categories and norms this "witness of transformation" would uphold with reference to power and authority of black women to create change by offering overt resistance to oppression. Asante regards the vital connection between personal commitment to the Afrocentric idea and the task of collective renewal and reconstruction as a significant mode of validation. He exhorts Afrocentrists to:

> Isolate, define, and promote those values, symbols, and experiences which affirm you. Only through this type of affirmation can we really and truly find our renewal; this is why I speak of it as a reconstruction instead of a redefinition. Actually what we have to do is not difficult because the guidelines are clearly established in our past. We must continue to be excellent, provocative, organized, educated, and dependable. . . . Afrocentricity does not condone inefficiency in its name. Our history gives us enough examples to illustrate this point. Those who have truly acted from their own Afrocentric centers have always had admirable records of excellence and efficiency.[8]

To summarize this brief analysis of the validation process as it operates in Afrocentric and womanist thought in terms of the threefold witness of Spirit, history, and transformation, it is clear that both paradigms offer distinct alternatives to traditional Eurocentric epistemologies. While neither paradigm would validate Eurocentric claims based upon the application of its own "witnessing" criteria, it seems evident that womanists might reject some expressions of Afrocentrism that are not centered upon the affirmation, assertiveness, and actualization of women. By the same token, one would expect some Afrocentrists to dismiss the womanist concept and to devalue the history of African American female leadership, as having only marginal significance as witnesses to the spirit, history, and transformative power of Afrocentrism.

Black Feminist Epistemology and Theological Education

Notwithstanding the apparent disparities and discrepancies inherent in paradigms centered exclusively in black women's experiences or in African American experiences without giving attention to gender distinctions, black feminist theorist Patricia Hill Collins has attempted to construct a coherent black feminist epistemology by merging Afrocentrist and feminist perspectives. Her discussion of the validation of black feminist claims in a 1989 article entitled "The Social Construction of Black Feminist Thought" invites application of the criteria of the witness of the Spirit, of history, and of transformation as indicated in this brief quotation:

> First, Black feminist thought must be validated by ordinary African-American women who grow to womanhood "in a world where the saner you are, the madder you are made to appear." To be credible in the eyes of this group, scholars must be personal advocates for their material, be accountable for the consequences of their work, have lived or experienced their material in some fashion, and be willing to engage in dialogues about their findings with ordinary, everyday people.[9]

Moreover, she requires acceptance by the community of black women scholars and at least confrontation, if not also constructive dialogue, with Eurocentric masculinist academia. She further suggests that if the validation of black feminist ideas as true becomes possible for African American women, African American men, white men, white women, and other groups with distinctive standpoints, with each group using the epistemological approaches growing from its unique standpoint, then black feminists may have found a route to the elusive goal of generating so-called objective generalizations that can stand as universal truths.[10]

In her discussion of the contours of an Afrocentric feminist epistemology, Patricia Hill Collins cites four elements: (1) concrete experience as a criterion of meaning, (2) the use of dialogue in assessing knowledge claims, (3) the ethic of caring, and (4) the ethic of personal accountability. Although all four elements find expression within the black church context, Collins uses the black church to further illustrate three components of the ethic of caring—the value placed on individual expressiveness, the appropriateness of emotions, and the capacity for empathy.[11] She arrives at a somewhat problematic conclusion regarding the ethic-of-care dimension of Afrocentric feminist epistemology:

> Although Black women may be denigrated within white-male-controlled academic institutions, other institutions, such as Black families and churches, which encourage the expression of Black female power, seem to do so by way of their support for an Afrocentric feminist epistemology.[12]

Because she fails to address the denigration of black women and the refutation of black female power in some black churches and families, Collins claims support for Afrocentric feminism in the very places where the rejection of these ideals is most noticeable. The difficulty inherent in the attempt to use this approach as a basis for denoting the convergence of Afrocentric and feminist values is grounded in the very important question of whether black churches and families can be generally described as Afrocentric, womanist, or neither of the above. However, even if Collins has erred by overstating the case for the black church and family as contexts for the emergence of Afrocentric feminist ideas, her epistemological analysis provides a useful point of departure for evaluation, in broad strokes, of the importance of Afrocentrist and womanist pedagogies for theological education. Indeed, her work may provide more specific indications for the task of educating persons for ministry to churches, families, and communities than the contributions of either Asante or Walker, given their apparent lack of specific interest in either Christianity or the black church.

The notion of concrete experience as a criterion of meaning, the use of dialogue in assessing knowledge claims, the ethic of caring, and the ethic of personal accountability promise to give new direction and content to theological curricula that take seriously the need to prepare men and women for the task of administering healing and wholeness in American society generally, and in the African American community in particular. We must not lose sight of the fact that many teachers and administrators in theological education today have yet to acknowledge the efforts undertaken by African American women and men to embrace Afrocentrism and/or womanism as paradigms for meaningful self-affirmation, self-assertion, and self-actualization. Moreover, many remain unaware of the extent to which the dominant epistemologies do not evoke the witness of the Spirit in the experience of the students, the witness of history in relation to traditions they recognize and care about, nor the witness of transformation for persons seeking to be equipped for and engaged in the work of interpersonal enablement and social transformation. Students who are preparing themselves for advanced scholarship or pastoral leadership can benefit greatly from being taught "how to" employ concrete experience as a criterion for meaning, and "how to" use dialogue in assessing knowledge claims, especially in their biblical, historical, and homiletical studies. The ethic of caring and the ethic of personal accountability not only should be central to the study of ethics and pastoral care, but also should have a direct bearing on how and why we do theology and religious education. It would be a mistake to view the pedagogical implications of the Afrocentric or womanist epistemologies as uniquely applicable to theological educating by and for African American people. While black theological institutions with significant numbers of female students should be held expressly responsible to give serious consideration to shaping their curricular offerings to reflect these concerns, predominantly white institutions might also find themselves revitalized by the process of intentionally seeking opportunities to enable the sharing of experiences and engagement in dialogue with African American women and men, in authentic contexts of mutual caring and accountability.

Afrocentric Challenges to Black Theological Education

Molefi Asante has engaged in dialogue with black religious scholars and leaders on several occasions, notably at the Society for the Study of Black Religion in 1993 and the Biblical Institute for Social Change in 1992. In his writings, however, he questions the usefulness of both Christianity and Islam to African peoples:

> The most crippling effect of Islam as well as Christianity for us may well be the adoption of non-African customs and behaviors, some of which are in direct conflict with our traditional values. We out Arab the Arabs as we have out Europeanized the Europeans from time to time. This is not so with the Afrocentrist. . . . We have a formidable history, replete with the voice of God, the ancestors, and the prophets. Our manner of dress, behavior, walk, talk and values are intact and workable when we are Afrocentric. Our problems come when we lose sight of ourselves,

accept false doctrines, false gods, mistaken notions of what is truly in our history, and assume an individualistic, antihumanistic and autocratic posture. . . . The dispensing with symbols and scriptures which stand outside of us is a move toward national recovery.[13]

Asante's understanding of Afrocentricity over against Christianity, Islam, and Marxism allows for tolerance and acceptance of Christians, Muslims, and Marxists of African descent. The question that must be openly and carefully addressed within theological education is whether the symbols and Scriptures of Christianity stand outside or within the history and experience of African peoples. Asante asserts that it is problematic for African Americans to accept mistaken notions of what is truly in our history, and on this basis to assume a dehumanizing posture in relation to others. This insight suggests guidelines and boundaries for Afrocentric dialogue within theological education, commencing when the Afrocentric Christian (or Muslim or Marxist, for that matter) comes to grips with the validation of his or her religion or ideology in light of Afrocentric ideals and criteria. One is challenged to decide whether one's true center of identity is African or Christian and then to take that stand without alienation or ambivalence. The alternative Asante prefers is to have African peoples acquire a new religious identity by way of *Njia*, or "the Way," a religious tradition he has constructed based on his own philosophical appropriation of the African spiritual heritage and history. The Way is apparently a revelation Asante received of 249 principles and proverbs organized in the form of 10 quarters. The first 10 are quoted here as a sampling of the content of its teachings:

1.   This is The Way that came to Molefi in America.
2.   The person who wishes death, attains it.

3. The person who wishes life, attains it.
4. All else is neither guidance nor religion.
5. Feeling is before belief and to everyone who feels is given belief.
6. A religion of the head brings dogma; feeling brings life.
7. Rejoice in The Way because it is right to rejoice in happiness.
8. The Way is not contradictory to Hinduism, Judaism, Christianity, Islam, Yoruba, or any other way of peace and power; it is complementary.
9. It comes last in the revelations; thus it builds upon previous foundations.
10. The Way is rooted in historical experiences and exists because it is spoken.[14]

Asante offers the Way as revealed knowledge, and it is important to note his insistence that it complements Christianity, Islam, Judaism, and Yoruba (presumably representing African traditional religion). Thus an open invitation to ecumenical engagement in the truth-seeking process is extended to African American theological educators and religious leaders committed to the Afrocentric idea. Asante has raised several crucial questions deserving of serious attention in black theological education. Which Christian symbols and Scriptures stand "outside us," and on what grounds are such judgments to be made? What is the role of racial and cultural factors in the validation of religious knowledge? Does the Christian confession necessarily obliterate or invalidate racial and cultural identity? Is there any correspondence between Asante's move toward national "recovery" and the Christian mandate to move toward reconciliation? Given that the ultimate objective of his method is to "transform human reality by ushering in a human openness to cultural pluralism which cannot exist without the unlocking of the minds for acceptance of an expansion of consciousness," it is clear that the scope of his endeavor can be inclusive of persons of all races, cultures, and nationalities, not just those of African descent.[15] It seems that, in Afrocentric perspective, the ideal of reconciliation bears the precise meaning of overcoming barriers of race, class, and sex to the extent that these hinder persons and communities from the mutual pursuit of well-being and wholeness.

Yosef ben-Jochannan has put forth a much more forceful and detailed critique of Christianity, Islam, and black theological education in his 1978 book *Our Black Seminarians and Black Clergy without a Black Theology*. His statement departs significantly from Asante's constructive Afrocentric ecumenics both in sentiment and tone, and directly confronts black theological educators with the case for a black theology based upon black gods reflecting the image of African peoples. The book begins with ben-Jochannan reporting his findings based upon visits to several black seminaries in the United States:

> I was more than disappointed; I was in fact disgusted. Let me hasten to add that my disgust was not caused by the APATHY of those at the helm of the SEMINARY, for such would be far from the truth in either case. The ironic insult is in the fact that not a solitary one of them *had*, *has*, and apparently if left alone *will ever have in the future*, its own BLACK THEOLOGY. Quite to the contrary, they—each and every one of them—have *adopted*, *accepted* and *perfected* a WHITE THEOLOGY with its WHITE HOLY FAMILY that includes their LILY WHITE BLONDE, BLUE EYE, GOLDEN HAIRED and DOVE OF PEACE passive *Jesus "the Christ."* Yet all of them maintained in their TEACHINGS and PREACHINGS from pulpits located directly under stained glass windows and wall-panels with their radiant exhibit of Michaelangelo's LILY WHITE HOLY FAMILY (comprised of his own UNCLE, AUNT-IN-LAW and COUSIN he used for the models he painted . . .) that:

> "GOD (meaning *Jesus* "*the Christ*") HAS NO COLOR."
>
> But if "*God Has No Color*," why does each new and/or existing panel and stained glass window in each and every "NEGRO/COLORED SEMINARY" wind up with the same type of LILY WHITE JESUS, ANGELS and HEAVEN . . . all of which is equally portrayed in each and every CHURCH headed by each and every "NEGRO/COLORED" graduate seminarian from each and every "NEGRO/COLORED" seminary?[16]

Ben-Jochannan's lament of the "brainwashing" of black seminarians continues with three complaints: (1) "very seldom, if ever, 'Negro Clergymen/women' quote 'Black Theologians' works," (2) he could not "find a solitary SERMON by a single BLACK clergyman or clergywoman held in equal esteem" as white preachers, and (3) "in most of the so-called 'NEGRO/ COLORED SEMINARIES' there still appear in the HYMNALS they use for 'DEVOTIONAL SINGING' songs with the following words: 'LORD, MAKE ME WHITER THAN SNOW.' "[17] The celebrative, critical, and constructive dimensions of ben-Jochannan's Afrocentric approach to theological education would require, respectively, worship and study of the ancient African gods; elimination of all vestiges of white supremacist Christianity in icons, images, hymns, sermons, and theology; and construction of a black theology that black people will understand, embrace, and respect. Particularly noteworthy is his inclusion of black women in the critique as persons whose theology and preaching ought to be held in high esteem, and also as among those held accountable to black norms. Ben-Jochannan's racial exclusivity is not also sexist, i.e., it does not convey a corresponding bias against women. In this regard he may be more "womanist" in his thinking than Asante. Although ben-Jochannan does not present an Afrocentric religious revelation in the manner of

Asante, his prescription for construction of this black theology does take the form of ten "commandments," which are exhortations toward the research, recovery, and restoration of Africa's "stolen legacy" in the form of religious and ethical ideas and texts, primarily from ancient Egypt.[18] Ben-Jochannan then spells out Seven Steps representing a method or approach for constructing a corrected black theology, briefly summarized as follows:

(1)   a presentation of AFRICAN RELIGIONS, GODS and GODDESSES;

(2)   a detailed analysis of the "SPIRIT WORLD" involved in our so-called "ANCESTRAL WORSHIP";

(3)   field trips to *the actual land*, and *amongst the indigenous Africans* of the specific religion and theology we are examining;

(4)   *the development of an archive of documents and other artifacts*, besides and including visual and oral aids (video tapes and recorded tapes);

(5)   *guest lectures* by the indigenous "AUTHORITIES" in each religion we examine;

(6)   *an honest analysis of all of the God-Heads* with complementary allegories and mythologies surrounding their creation and birth; and

(7)   *research and writing cadres* to analyze the available materials and artifacts used in Judaeo-Christian and Islamic THEOSOPHY and THEOLOGY with respect to (African) PHILOSOPHICAL MYSTICISM.[19]

Although ben-Jochannan does not name Howard School of Divinity in his survey, in several ways his critique pertains directly to Howard, notwithstanding our past and present efforts to incorporate Afrocentric perspectives into the curriculum. Some elements of ben-Jochannan's "ten commandments" and "seven steps" have been embraced by Howard faculty in our individual and collective research efforts, particularly in the study of the history of religions and biblical literature, language, and hermeneutics. Black theology and black preaching are held in high esteem at Howard, as evidenced by the curriculum, course syllabi, public lectures, other special events, and the extensive collection of books, cassettes, and videotapes on black theology and preaching in the Divinity Library. Although hymnals from various Christian traditions have been made available as worship aids in Thurman Chapel, no effort has been made to expunge songs or hymnals that make reference to being washed "white as snow," including hymnals published by the black churches. White images of the divine are predominant in the art and architecture of Benjamin E. Mays Hall, formerly Holy Name College, a Franciscan monastery acquired and refurbished by Howard University in the mid-1980s. None of the white icons put in place by the Franciscans have been removed or altered; moreover, a gift of Greek icons was received in 1992 and put on display in a special gallery. Yet there are some prominent displays of black religious art. An oil painting hanging in the reception area depicting the baptism of the Ethiopian by Philip as described in Acts 8:26–40 was commissioned at the time of the School's dedication in 1987 and painted by an alumna of the School of Divinity, Mrs. Bessie Downing. Also, a collection of photographic images of black madonnas (posed with a white infant Jesus!) and other religious scenes are exhibited outside Thurman Chapel, accompanied by the following inscription:

> Madonnas in Art with Ave Marias in Music originated at Andrew Rankin Memorial Chapel, Howard University, as one of the Worship through the Arts Series. . . . The productions were created under the general direction of

Howard Thurman, who was Dean of Rankin Chapel
from 1932 to 1944. . . . The subjects were chosen from
the undergraduate student body of the University.

In 1993 the Andre Tweed Collection featuring religious artifacts from ancient Ethiopia was dedicated as a permanent ex-
hibition. Other art displays in various media depict black religious
leaders deemed worthy of special honor at the School of Divinity: Nannie Helen Burroughs, Joseph Jackson, Benjamin
Mays, and Howard Thurman. The religious art, images, and
hymnody of the School of Divinity would not satisfy the exclusive Afrocentric criteria posited by ben-Jochannan, but
rather are more reflective of the ecumenical Afrocentric ideal
ascribed by Asante. While little or no effort has been made to
purge the hymnals and liturgies of gender-exclusive language,
women are fairly well represented in the images displayed
around the school, both as artists and as subjects.

These two alternate approaches to Afrocentric theological
study, Asante's "ecumenical" Afrocentricity and ben-Jochannan's "exclusive" Afrocentricity, both reject Christianity,
which is of course the dominant religious tradition within
black theological education and religious institutions. Ben-
Jochannan's more negative critique is nevertheless helpful as
an impetus to scrutinize the major issues at stake when one
commits to an Afrocentric mode of religious study and practice. Does the rejection and even ridicule of Christianity by
some Afrocentrists render the Afrocentric perspective irrel-
evant to theological education in this country? If so, can we at
least respond to the critical questions and concerns, if we
cannot also embrace the vision and constructs? In other
words, even if the dialogue begins and ends with the attempt
to respond to the Afrocentric agenda from a Christian perspective, and stops short of appropriating the full complement

of Afrocentric ideas, images, symbols, and myths, black theological students and educators would do well to take Afrocentricity seriously as a vantage point for organizing our thinking about the study of religion in order to become better prepared for ministry among and in partnership with African American people. Although their choice of words seems to set them apart, when Asante speaks of "unlocking" minds and "expansion" of consciousness, on the one hand, and ben-Jochannan laments the "brainwashing" of black seminarians, on the other, the two are addressing the same point: that African Americans suffer serious and debilitating deficiencies in perspective regarding Africa in relation to the world. By implication, then, it is the express role and responsibility of black theological educators and black clergy to correct these deficiencies in our own thinking so that we can be more effective as teachers, preachers, and leaders in the task of enlightening the people we serve with respect to the truth about Africa and themselves.

A Critical Mass

The womanist idea has found a home among African American women who are engaged in theological study as teachers and students. In particular, the Howard University School of Divinity has been a leading forum for the development of womanist scholarship, beginning in 1985 with the institution of the Feminine in Religious Traditions Lecture Series, including the 1988 Consultation of Womanist Scholars in Religion, and continuing with a steady stream of articles by and about womanist theologians and pastors in the school's *Journal of Religious Thought* since 1986.[20]

    In the final analysis, it may be that neither Afrocentric nor womanist approaches will find wide acceptance in the Christian churches in general, or in black churches. A key factor in determining such an outcome, however, would be whether a critical mass of African American female students and theological faculty can embrace and integrate these two concepts on several levels: (1) as points of departure for engaging in scholarship and ministry consistently in an Afrocentric womanist frame of reference; (2) as sources of content and method in theological and ministerial studies in conjunction with or in place of traditional Western sources; (3) as organizing principles for ministry in the churches and community; (4) as foundations for cultural values and aesthetic norms applied to everyday life, e.g., diet, decor, clothing, hairstyles; (5) as perspectives for framing thought and action with regard to various life choices, including educational pursuits, career paths, marriage, family and sexual partnerships, management of human and material resources (i.e., how we earn, spend, and invest our money), political activity, and community-building; (6) as centers of personal and social identity vital to our sense of call and response to ministry; and (7) as grounds for envisioning the future toward which we work and hope. It is the testimony of increasing numbers of African American women in theological education that the witness of the Spirit, of history, and of transformation encourages worship, study, and work in an Afrocentric womanist context. The development of African American women's religious leadership in this light promises to equip the churches better to love black people to wholeness.

Notes

Introduction

1. For Alice Walker's definition, see *In Search of Our Mothers' Gardens: Womanist Prose* (New York: Harcourt Brace Jovanovich, 1983), xi–xii.

2. Molefi Kete Asante, *Afrocentricity* (Trenton, N.J.: Africa World Press, 1988), 6.

3. This way of describing the multiple oppression that besets African American women is taken from Patricia Hill Collins's *Black Feminist Thought* (New York: Routledge, 1991).

4. Molefi Kete Asante, *Kemet, Afrocentricity and Knowledge* (Trenton, N.J.: Africa World Press, 1990), 9–10.

1. We Have a Beautiful Mother

1. Deborah K. King, "Multiple Jeopardy, Multiple Consciousness: The Context of a Black Feminist Ideology," in Micheline R. Malson *et. al.*, eds., *Black Women in America* (Chicago: Univ. of Chicago Press, 1988), 270.

2. For background and discussion of the Moynihan report on "The Negro Family," see Lee Rainwater and William L. Yancey, *The Moynihan Report and the Politics of Controversy* (Cambridge, Mass.: M.I.T. Press, 1976); also Cheryl Townsend Gilkes, "Letter to the Editor," *New York Times*, December 26, 1993. E. Franklin Frazier's classic text is *The Negro Family in the United States* (Chicago: Univ. of Chicago Press, 1939).

3. See W. E. B. DuBois, *The Souls of Black Folk* (Millwood, N.Y.: Kraus Thomson, 1973 [1903]), esp. the chapter "Of Our Spiritual Striving." Also pertinent is DuBois's later work in *The Gift of Black Folk: The Negro and the Making of America* (Millwood, N.Y.: Kraus Thomason, 1975 [1924]).

4. (Dallas: S.M.U. Press, 1975 [reprint of 1963 edition]).

5. See George G. James, *Stolen Legacy: The Greeks Were Not the Authors of Greek Philosophy but the People of North Africa, Commonly Called the Egyptians* (San Francisco: Julian Richardson Assocs., 1988 [1954]).

6. Molefi Kete Asante, *Afrocentricity* (Trenton, N.J.: Africa World Press, 1988); *idem, The Afrocentric Idea* (Philadelphia: Temple Univ. Press, 1987).

7. Among Diop's works are Cheikh A. Diop, *The African Origin of Civilization: Myth or Reality?* ed. and trans. Mercer Cook (Brooklyn: Lawrence Hill Books, 1974); *Black Africa: The Economic and Cultural Basis for a Federated State* (rev. ed.; Brooklyn: Lawrence Hill Books, 1987); *The Cultural Unity of Black Africa* (2d ed.; Chicago: Third World Press, 1987).

8. Nathan Glazer, "The Issue of Cultural Pluralism in America Today," in Joseph A. Ryan, ed., *White Ethnics: Their Life in Working-Class America* (Englewood Cliffs, N.J.: Prentice Hall, 1973).

9. Allan Bloom, *The Closing of the American Mind* (New York: Simon & Schuster, 1987); Arthur M. Schlesinger, Jr., *The Disuniting of America* (New York: W. W. Norton, 1992).

10. James Baldwin, "On Being White and Other Lies," *Essence*, April 1984, 90–94.

11. See Frank M. Snowden, Jr., *Before Color Prejudice: The Ancient View of Blacks* (Cambridge, Mass.: Harvard Univ. Press, 1983); *idem, Blacks in Antiquity: Ethiopians in the Greco-Roman Experience* (Cambridge, Mass.: Belknap Press, 1970).

12. Robert E. Hood, *Must God Remain Greek? Afro Cultures and God-Talk* (Minneapolis: Fortress Press, 1990).

13. See Henry Lewis Gates, Jr., "Whose Canon Is It, Anyway?" *New York Times Book Review*, Feb. 26, 1989; reprinted in *idem, Loose Canons: Notes on the Culture Wars* (N.Y.: Oxford Univ. Press, 1992).

14. Alice Walker, *In Search of Our Mothers' Gardens: Womanist Prose* (San Diego: Harcourt Brace Jovanovich, 1983).

15. (San Diego: Harcourt Brace Jovanovich, 1989).

16. Patricia Hill Collins, *Black Feminist Thought* (New York: Routledge, 1991), 38.

17. Ibid., 39.

2. Afrocentrism and Male-Female Relations

1. Kariamu Welsh, "Foreword," in Molefi Kete Asante, *Afrocentricity* (Trenton, N.J.: Africa World Press, 1988), vii.

2. Asante, *Afrocentricity*, 26.

3. Ibid., 27.

4. Ibid., 36.

5. Ibid., 52.

6. Ibid., 52.

7. See bell hooks, *Ain't I a Woman?* (Boston: South End Press, 1970).

8. See Michele Wallace, *Black Macho and the Myth of the Superwoman* (New York: Dial Press, 1979).

9. Asante, *Afrocentricity*, 52.

10. Ibid., 53.

11. Ibid., 54.

12. Ibid., 56.

13. Asante defines afrology as "the Afrocentric study of concepts, issues, and behaviors with particular bases in the African world, diasporan and continental. Black Studies, African Studies and African-American Studies are essentially afrological studies, that is, persons within departments or programs with such names are usually engaged in the Afrocentric study of concepts, issues and behaviors in the African world." See his book, *Afrocentricity*, 58–64.

14. Ibid., 63–64.

15. Chinua Achebe, *Things Fall Apart* (New York: Fawcett, 1995).

16. Buchi Emecheta, *The Joys of Motherhood* (New York: G. Braziller, 1979).

17. Awa Thiam, *Black Sisters, Speak Out* (London: Pluto Press, 1986, reprinted 1991).

18. See Awa Thiam's account of the origins and current practices of excision and infibulation in *Black Sisters, Speak Out*, 58–87.

19.   Margaret Walker, *For My People* (New Haven, Conn.: Yale Univ. Press, 1942).

20.   Asante, *Afrocentricity*, 73.

21.   Ibid., 77.

22.   Ibid., 71.

23.   Ibid., 75.

24.   Ibid., 76–77.

25.   Ibid., 77.

3. A Womanist Response to the Afrocentric Idea

1.   Alice Walker, *In Search of Our Mothers' Gardens: Womanist Prose* (New York: Harcourt Brace Jovanovich, 1983), xi–xii.

2.   Molefi Kete Asante, *Afrocentricity* (Trenton, N.J.: African World Press, 1988), 2.

3.   Ibid., 2.

4.   Ibid., 1.

5.   Walker, *In Search*, xi–xii.

6.   Delores S. Williams, "Womanist Theology: Black Women's Voices," *Christianity and Crisis* (March 2, 1987):66–70.

7.   Jacquelyn Grant, "Womanist Theology: Black Women's Experience as a Source for Doing Theology, with Special Reference to Christology," *Journal of the Interdenominational Theological Center* 13, 2 (Spring 1986): 199.

8.   Jarena Lee, *The Life and Spiritual Experiences of Jarena Lee*, in William L. Andrews, ed., *Sisters of the Spirit: Three Black Women's Autobiographies of the 19th Century* (Bloomington: Indiana Univ. Press, 1986), 36.

9.   Luke 10:42 (NRSV).

10.   Lee, *Life*, 36.

11.   Cheryl Townsend Gilkes, "The Role of Women in the Sanctified Church," *Journal of Religious Thought* 43 (Spring-Summer 1986): 24.

12.   Michelle Briggs, "Black Women Free to Choose," in Henry J. Young, ed., *God and Human Freedom* (Marynoll, N.Y.: Orbis Books, 1979), 71.

13. Katie G. Cannon, "Unctuousness as Virtue, according to the Life of Zora Neale Hurston," *Journal of Feminist Studies in Religion* (Spring 1985): 38.

14. Katie G. Cannon, "Hitting a Straight Lick with a Crooked Stick: The Womanist Dilemma in the Development of a Black Liberation Ethic," *Annual of the Society of Christian Ethics* (1987), 168.

15. Lee, *Life*, 37.

16. Isaiah 40:31 (NRSV).

17. Lee, *Life*, 36.

18. Asante, *Afrocentricity*, xi.

19. Lee, *Life*, 36.

20. Walker, *In Search*, xi–xii.

4. To Reflect the Image of God

1. Alice Walker, *In Search of Our Mothers' Gardens: Womanist Prose* (New York: Harcourt Brace Jovanovich, 1983), xi.

2. The phrase *interlocking system of oppression* comes from sociologist Patricia Hill Collins's depiction of African American women's oppression. See *Black Feminist Thought: Knowledge, Consciousness, and the Politics of Empowerment* (New York: Routledge, 1991), 44.

3. Cheryl Townsend Gilkes, "The 'Loves' and 'Troubles' of African-American Women's Bodies: The Womanist Challenge to Cultural Humiliation and Community Ambivalence," in Emilie M. Townes, ed., *A Troubling in My Soul: Womanist Perspectives on Evil and Suffering* (Maryknoll, N.Y.: Orbis Books, 1993), 237.

4. Collins, *Black Feminist Thought*, 44.

5. Ibid., 49.

6. Angela Davis, *Women, Race, and Class* (New York: Random House, 1981), 8–9.

7. John W. Blassingame, ed., *Slave Testimony* (Baton Rouge: Louisiana State Univ. Press, 1977), 133.

8. Ibid., 130.

9. Ibid., 133.

10. Deborah Gray White, *Ar'n't I a Woman: Female Slaves in the Plantation South* (New York: W. W. Norton and Co., 1985).

11.   Jacqueline Jones, *Labor of Love, Labor of Sorrow* (New York: Basic Books, 1985), 41.

12.   White, *Ar'n't I a Woman*, 158.

13.   Cited in Miriam Schneir, ed., *Feminism: The Essential Historical Writings* (New York: Vintage Books, 1972), 93.

5.   Slavery as a Sacred Text

1.   Alice Walker, *The Color Purple* (New York: Washington Square Press, 1982), 176.

2.   Jarena Lee, *The Life and Spiritual Experiences of Jarena Lee*, in William L. Andrews, ed., *Sisters of the Spirit: Three Black Women's Autobiographies of the 19th Century* (Bloomington: Indiana Univ. Press, 1986), 36.

3.   Ibid.

4.   Delores S. Williams, "*The Color Purple*: What Was Missed," *Christianity and Crisis* (July 14, 1986), 231.

5.   Toni Morrison, *Song of Solomon* (New York: Signet, 1977), 18–19.

6.   M. M. Bahktin, *The Dialogic Imagination*, ed. Michael Holquist (Austin: Univ. of Texas Press, 1981), 424.

7.   Ibid.

8.   Ibid.

9.   Ralph Ellison, *et al.*, "The Uses of History in Fiction," in *The Southern Literary Journal* 1 (Spring 1969): 60.

10.   Bernard W. Bell, *The Afro-American Novel and Its Tradition* (Amherst: Univ. of Massachusetts Press, 1987), 289. Henry Louis Gates terms the form the "slave narrative novel." See "The Language of Slavery," his introduction to *The Slave's Narrative*, ed. Charles Davis and Henry L. Gates, Jr. (New York: Oxford Univ. Press, 1985).

11.   Of course, there were novels of slavery published before the 1860s, but, in terms of sheer numbers, it is a subject engaged by far more authors in this century. Nineteenth-century novels of slavery include the major antebellum novels—William Wells Brown, *Clotel; or the President's Daughter: A Narrative of Slave Life in the United States* (1853); Martin Delaney, *Blake; or the Huts of America* (1859); Harriet E. Wilson, *Our Nig* (1859); James Howard, *Bond and Free* (1866); and, though not focused exclusively on slavery,

Frances E. W. Harper, *Iola Leroy* (1892). Twentieth-century examples include Arna Bontemps's historical romances: *Black Thunder* (1936) and *Drums at Dusk* (1939). See Hazel Carby's essay, "Ideologies of Black Folk: Novels of Slavery and Sharecropping in the 20th Century," for a discussion of what she describes as "the apparent centrality of slavery to the literary imagination despite the relatively few novels of slavery."

12. Recent novels about slavery include Ernest Gaines, *The Autobiography of Miss Jane Pittman* (1971); Ishmael Reed, *Flight to Canada* (1976); Barbara Chase-Riboud, *Sally Hemings* (1979); Octavia Butler, *Kindred* (1979); Charles Johnson, *The Oxherding Tale* (1982); Sherley Anne Williams, *Dessa Rose* (1984), and Toni Morrison, *Beloved* (1987). Even recent novels by African Americans that don't focus on the slave experience, or use it as a significant point of departure, stage their character's necessary confrontation with some story about slavery. Examples include Avey in Paule Marshall, *Praisesong for the Widow* (1983) and Ursa in Gayl Jones, *Corregidora* (1975).

13. For a general survey of the history of these warring interpretations, see William L. Van Deburg, *Slavery and Race in American Popular Culture* (Madison: Univ. of Wisconsin Press, 1984).

14. See Charles Rowell, "Poetry, History and Humanism: Interview with Margaret Walker," in *Black World* (December 1975), 10.

15. Sherley Anne Williams, Author's Note to *Dessa Rose* (New York: William Morrow, 1986), 5. Parenthetical references in text hereafter refer to page numbers in this volume.

16. The controversy surrounding Styron's novel was widespread among black writers and intellectuals, most of whom maintained that Styron's *created* Nat Turner bore little resemblance to the *actual* historical figure. See *William Styron's Nat Turner: Ten Black Writers Respond*, ed. John Henrik Clarke (Boston: Beacon Press, 1968). For a critique of Styron's critics, see Seymour L. Gross and Eileen Bender, "History, Politics and Literature: The Myth of Nat Turner," in *American Quarterly* 23 (October 1971):487–518.

17. A version of the first section of *Dessa Rose* was entitled "Meditations on History"—no doubt an act of signifying on Styron—which appeared in *Midnight Birds: Stories of Contemporary Black Women Writers* (New York: Doubleday Anchor, 1980), 200–48.

18. See "Using the Testimony of Ex-Slaves: Approaches and Problems," in Davis and Gates, *The Slave's Narrative*, 83.

19. Frances Foster notes importantly that in published slave narratives by black women, their sexual abuse is noticeably de-emphasized. She observes that they "never present rape or seduction as the most profound aspect of their existence." See " 'In Respect to Females. . . ': Differences in the Portrayals of Women by Male and Female Narrators," in *Black American Literature Forum* 15 (Summer 1981): 67.

20. Kimberly Benston, "I yam, what I am: the Topos of Un-(naming) in Afro-American Literature," in *Black Literature and Literary Theory*, ed. Henry Louis Gates, Jr. (New York: Methuen, 1984), 157.

21. Williams also uses architectural space/place to ironize and mock Nehemiah's assumed superiority, for his "Big House" is a run-down farmhouse in which he has an " 'attic half' that was little better than a loft" (26), a far cry from the "Great Houses" of Cavalier, Virginia, that had once opened their doors to him.

22. I borrow this phrase from Margaret A. Simons, "Racism and Feminism: A Schism in the Sisterhood," in *Feminist Studies* 5 (Summer 1979): 384–401.

23. For a discussion of the feminist interrogation and critique of gender-linked vision, see Craig Owens, "The Discourse of Others: Feminists and Postmodernism," in *The Anti-Aesthetic: Essays on Post-Modern Culture*, ed. Hal Foster (Port Townsend, Wash.: Bay Press, 1983), 57–77; see especially 70–77.

24. Bahktin, *The Dialogic Imagination*, 424.

25. William L. Andrews, *To Tell a Free Story: The First Century of Afro-American Autobiography, 1760–1865* (Urbana: Univ. of Illinois Press, 1986), 14.

26. Henri Bergson, *Comedy* (New York: Doubleday, 1956), 121–22.

27. Toni Morrison, interview by Charlayne Hunter-Gault, "MacNeil/Lehrer Report," September 29, 1987.

6. Living in the Intersection

1. Quoted in Sandi Russell, *Render Me My Song: African-American Women Writers from Slavery to the Present* (New York: St. Martin's Press, 1990), 8.

2. Earlene Stetson, ed., *Black Sister: Poetry by Black American Women, 1746–1980* (Bloomington: Indiana Univ. Press, 1981), xix.

3. Ibid., xv.

4. Claudia Tate, ed., *Black Women Writers at Work* (New York: Continuum, 1983), xvii.

5. Gloria Wade-Gayles, *No Crystal Stair: Visions of Race and Sex in Black Women's Fiction* (New York: Pilgrim Press, 1984), 20.

6. Tate, ed., *Black Women Writers*, xvi.

7. Katie G. Cannon, *Black Womanist Ethics* (Atlanta: Scholars Press, 1988), 5.

8. Russell, *Render*, 93.

9. Ibid., 76.

10. Arthur P. Davis, *From the Dark Tower: Afro-American Writers, 1900–1960* (Washington, D.C.: Howard Univ. Press, 1981), 205.

11. Russell, *Render*, 97.

12. Ibid., 105.

13. Quoted in Tate, ed., *Black Women Writers*, 183.

14. Ibid., 185.

15. Stetson, *Black Sister*, xix.

16. Ibid., xxiii.

17. Ibid., xxi.

18. Alice Walker, *Revolutionary Petunias and Other Poems* (New York: Harcourt Brace Jovanovich, 1973), 57.

19. Maya Angelou, *Oh Pray My Wings Are Gonna Fit Me Well* (New York: Random House, 1975).

20. Quoted in Russell, *Render*, 131.

21. Ibid., 38.

22. Ibid., 149.

23. Tate, ed., *Black Women Writers*, 149.

24. Russell, *Render*, 142.

25. Satiafa, *For Dark Women and Others* (Detroit: Lotus Press, 1982), 2.

26. Ibid., 29.

27. Carolyn Rodgers, *how i got ovah: New and Selected Poems* (New York: Doubleday Anchor, 1968), 47.

28. Ibid., 50.

29. Tate, ed., *Black Women Writers*, 162.

30. Shange, "no more love poems #1," in *for colored girls who have considered suicide when the rainbow is enuf* (N.Y.: Macmillan, 1977), 42–43.

31. Walker, *Revolutionary Petunias*, 44.

32. Tate, ed., *Black Women Writers*, xxii.

33. Ibid., xx.

34. Russell, *Render*, 90.

35. Davis, *Dark Tower*, 142.

36. Russell, *Render*, 116.

37. Stetson, *Black Sister*, xvii.

38. Margaret Walker and Nikki Giovanni, *A Poetic Equation: Conversations between Nikki Giovanni and Margaret Walker* (Washington, D.C.: Howard Univ. Press, 1974), 91.

39. Tillie Olsen, "Foreword," in Tate, ed., *Black Women Writers*, x.

40. Tate, ed., *Black Women Writers*, xxii.

41. In Russell, *Render*, 83.

42. Gwendolyn Brooks, *Report from Part One* (Detroit: Broadside Press, 1972), 204.

43. Walker, *Revolutionary Petunias*, 30–31.

44. See Russell, *Render*, 131.

45. Gloria I. Joseph and Jill Lewis, *Common Differences: Conflicts in Black and White Feminist Perspectives* (Boston: South End Press, 1981), 28.

46. Wade-Gayles, *No Crystal Stair*, 230.

47. Quoted in Tate, ed., *Black Women Writers*, 153.

48. Joseph and Lewis, *Common Differences*, 27.

49. Tate, ed., *Black Women Writers*, 163.

50. Ibid., xvi.

51. Cannon, *Black Womanist Ethics*, 4.

52. Beverly Guy-Sheftall, *Daughters of Sorrow: Attitudes toward Black Women, 1880–1920* (New York: Carlson Pub., 1990), xiv.

53. Zillah Eisenstein, "A Personal Response," in Wade-Gayles, *No Crystal Stair*, xx.

54. Ibid., 217–20.

55. Langston Hughes, "Notes on Commercial Theatre," in *Selected Poems of Langston Hughes* (New York: Alfred A. Knopf, 1968), 190.

7. Black Women in Biblical Perspective

1. Phillis Wheatley, "The Black Beauty," quoted in William L. Van Deburg, *Slavery and Race in American Popular Culture* (Madison: Univ. of Wisconsin Press, 1984), 57.

2. Maria W. Stewart, "Mrs. Stewart's Farewell Address to Her Friends in the City of Boston," in Marilyn Richardson, ed., *Maria W. Stewart, America's First Black Woman Political Writer* (Bloomington: Indiana Univ. Press, 1987), 68.

3. Thomas L. Webber, *Deep Like the Rivers* (New York: W. W. Norton, 1978), 192.

4. Howard Thurman, *Jesus and the Disinherited* (Richmond, Ind.: Friends United Press, 1949, 1981), 30–31.

5. Zilpha Elaw, *Memoirs of the Life, Religious Experience, Ministerial Travels and Labours of Mrs. Zilpha Elaw, An American Female of Colour; Together with Some Account of the Great Religious Revivals in America* (London, 1846); Julia A. J. Foote, *A Brand Plucked from the Fire: An Autobiographical Sketch* (Cleveland: W. F. Schneider, 1879); Jarena Lee, *The Life and Religious Experience of Jarena Lee, A Coloured Lady, Giving an Account of Her Call to Preach the Gospel* (Philadelphia, 1836); Amanda Berry Smith, *An Autobiography: The Story of the Lord's Dealing with Mrs. Amanda Smith, The Colored Evangelist, Containing an Account of Her Life Work of Faith, and Her Travels in America, England, Ireland, Scotland, India, and Africa as an Independent Missionary* (Chicago: Meyer & Brother, 1893). Note that these women forthrightly identify themselves as women of color in these titles, with the exception of Foote. The Elaw, Foote, and Lee autobiographies are reprinted together with an informative introduction in William L. Andrews, ed., *Sisters of the Spirit* (Bloomington: Indiana Univ. Press, 1986). See also the article and corresponding documents in "Amanda Berry Smith: A 'Downright, Outright Christian'" by Nancy A. Hardesty and Adrienne Israel in Rosemary Skinner Keller, ed., *Spirituality and Social Responsibility* (Nashville: Abingdon Press, 1993).

6. Cited in Hardesty and Israel, "Amanda Berry Smith," 67.

7. Ibid., 68.

8. Cited in Andrews, *Sisters of the Spirit*, 209.

9.   Clarence G. Newsome, "Mary McLeod Bethune and the Methodist Episcopal Church North: In but Out," *Journal of Religious Thought* 49 (Summer-Fall 1992): 10.

10.   Evelyn Brooks Higginbotham, *Righteous Discontent: The Women's Movement in the Black Baptist Church* (Cambridge, Mass.: Harvard Univ. Press, 1993), 216.

11.   Nannie Helen Burroughs, "Roll Call of Bible Women," from Rosemary Radford Ruether and Rosemary Skinner Keller, eds., *Women and Religion in America*, vol. 3 (San Francisco: Harper & Row, 1986), 128.

12.   Marian Wright Edelman, *The Measure of Our Success* (Boston: Beacon Press, 1992), 76–78.

13.   Ella Pearson Mitchell, *Those Preachin' Women* (Valley Forge: Judson Press, 1985), *Those Preaching Women*, vol. 2 (Valley Forge: Judson Press, 1989), and *Women: To Preach or Not to Preach* (Valley Forge: Judson Press, 1991). For a comparative analysis of sermons preached by black women and men, see Cheryl J. Sanders, "Woman as Preacher," *Journal of Religious Thought* 43, 1 (Spring-Summer 1986): 6–23.

14.   See, e.g., Phyllis Trible, *God and the Rhetoric of Sexuality* (Philadelphia: Fortress Press, 1978); idem, *Texts of Terror: Literary-Feminist Readings of Biblical Narratives* (Philadelphia: Fortress Press, 1984); Elisabeth Schüssler Fiorenza, *In Memory of Her: A Feminist Theological Reconstruction of Christian Origins* (New York: Crossroad, 1984); idem, *But She Said: Feminist Practices of Biblical Interpretation* (Boston: Beacon Press, 1992).

15.   Katie G. Cannon, "The Emergence of Black Feminist Consciousness," in Letty M. Russell, ed., *Feminist Interpretation of the Bible* (Philadelphia: Westminster Press, 1985): 30–40.

16.   Renita J. Weems, *Just a Sister Away: A Womanist Vision of Women's Relationships in the Bible* (San Diego: LuraMedia, 1988); idem, *I Asked for Intimacy: Stories of Blessings, Betrayals, and Birthings* (San Diego: LuraMedia, 1993).

17.   (Decatur, Ga.: Scholars Press, 1989).

18.   (Minneapolis: Fortress Press, 1991). See also Cain Hope Felder's *Troubling Biblical Waters* (Maryknoll, N.Y.: Orbis Books, 1989).

19.   Delores S. Williams, *Sisters in the Wilderness: The Challenge of Womanist God-Talk* (Maryknoll, N.Y.: Orbis Books, 1993).

20. Alice O. Bellis, *Helpmates, Harlots, and Heroes: Women's Stories in the Hebrew Bible* (Louisville, Ky.: Westminster/John Knox Press, 1994).

8. Teaching Womanist Theology

1. See Paulo Friere, *Pedagogy of the Oppressed* (New York: Seabury Press, 1970), especially chap. 2.

2. For Alice Walker's definition, see *In Search of Our Mothers' Gardens: Womanist Prose* (New York: Harcourt Brace Jovanovich, 1983), xi–xii.

3. Patricia Hill Collins, *Black Feminist Thought: Knowledge, Consciousness, and the Politics of Empowerment* (New York: Routledge, 1991).

4. Audre Lorde, *Sister Outsider* (New York: Crossing Press Feminist Series, 1984), 45.

5. Collins, *Black Feminist Thought*, 31ff.

9. Afrocentric and Womanist Approaches to Theological Education

1. Molefi Asante, *The Afrocentric Idea* (Philadelphia: Temple Univ. Press, 1987), 195.

2. Alice Walker, *In Search of Our Mothers' Gardens: Womanist Prose* (San Diego: Harcourt Brace Jovanovich, 1983), xi–xii.

3. Asante, *The Afrocentric Idea*, 170.

4. Walker, *Our Mothers' Gardens*, 82.

5. Asante, *The Afrocentric Idea*, 17.

6. Ibid., 179.

7. Molefi Kete Asante, *Afrocentricity* (Trenton, N.J.: Africa World Press, 1988), 5–6.

8. Asante, *Afrocentricity*, 41.

9. Patricia Hill Collins, "The Social Construction of Black Feminist Thought," *Signs* 14 (Summer 1989): 771.

10. Ibid., 773.

11. Ibid., 767.

12. Ibid., 768.

13. Asante, *Afrocentricity*, 5–7.

14. Ibid., 109.

15. Molefi Asante, *Kemet, Afrocentricity and Knowledge* (Trenton, N.J.: Africa World Press, 1990), v.

16. Yosef A. A. ben-Jochannan, *Our Black Seminarians and Black Clergy without a Black Theology* (New York: Alkebu-lan Books, 1978), 1.

17. Ibid., 1–3.

18. Ibid., 25–40.

19. Ibid., 40–41.

20. See the following issues of the *Journal of Religious Thought* for published lectures from the Feminine in Religious Traditions Lecture Series: (1) *JRT* 43, 1 (Spring-Summer 1986): Delores Causion Carpenter, "The Professionalization of the Ministry of Women," Cheryl Townsend Gilkes, "The Role of Women in the Sanctified Church"; Cheryl J. Sanders, "The Woman as Preacher"; and Delores S. Williams, "The Color of Feminism: Or Speaking the Black Woman's Tongue"; (2) *JRT* 44, 2 (Winter-Spring 1988): Evelyn Brooks, "Religion, Politics and Gender: The Leadership of Nannie Helen Burroughs"; and Toinette Eugene, "Moral Values and Black Womanists"; (3) *JRT* 46, 1 (Summer-Fall 1989): Kelly D. Brown, "God Is as Christ Does: Toward a Womanist Theology"; and Harold Dean Trulear, "Reshaping Black Pastoral Theology: The Vision of Bishop Ida B. Robinson"; (4) *JRT* 49, 1 (Summer-Fall 1992): Clarence G. Newsome, "Mary McLeod Bethune and the Methodist Episcopal Church North: In but Out." See also *JRT* 45, 1 (Summer-Fall 1988): Jacqueline D. Carr-Hamilton, "Notes on the Black Womanist Dilemma"; and *JRT* 46, 2 (Winter-Spring 1989–1990). I have also pursued questions of the relationship of Afrocentricity and Christianity in my article "Afrocentricity and Theological Education," in the *Journal of Religious Thought* 50 (1994): 11–26.

Index

Achebe, C., 52, 179 n.15
Activists, black women, 16, 42, 126–28
Africa, 37, 39, 52, 69, 71, 109–10, 140, 157, 174
African queens, 48, 127, 139–41
Afrocentrism, Afrocentricity, 10, 26, 46, 59, 65–66, 106–7, 110, 157–59
Afrology, 51
AIDS, 44
Allen, R., 63, 124
American Academy of Religion, 12–13
Andrews, W., 98, 180 n.8, 184 n.25, 182 n.2, 187 n.58
Angelou, M., 16, 111, 185 n.19
Asante, M., 9, 15, 17, 30, 43, 45–54, 158–62, 166–68, 170–71, 173–74, 177 n.2, 178 n.6, 179 nn.2–6, 9–13; 180 nn.2–4, 20–25; 181 n.18, 189 nn.1, 3, 5–8; 190 nn.13, 15

Bahktin, M., 83–84, 182 nn.6, 7, 8; 184 n.24
Baldwin, J., 32–33, 178 n.10
Baraka, A., 44–45
Bell, B., 84, 182 n.16
Bellis, A., 130, 189 n.20
ben-Jochannan, Y., 17, 169–71, 173–74, 190 nn.16–19
Bergson, H., 99, 184 n.26
Bethune, M., 16, 127, 188 n.9, 190 n.20
Bible, 16, 126, 142, 149, 153
Bible names
Abram, Abraham, 131–33, 135–37, 142
Aaron, 139
Candace (Ethiopian Queen), 16, 127, 141
Cushite woman, 139
Deborah, 105, 122
Eden, 38
Esther, 105, 122
Ethiopian eunuch, 141, 172
Gershom, 138
Hagar, 16, 131–37, 142
Ishmael, 133, 135–36
Isaac, 133, 135
Jacob, 136
Jerusalem, 139–41
Joseph, 136–38
Mary Magdalene, 105, 122
Miriam, 139
Moses, 138–39, 142
Noah, 82
Queen of Sheba, 16, 139–41

Sarah, Sarai, 131–33, 136
Solomon, 139–42
Woman in Song of Solomon, 122
Zipporah, 16, 138–39
Bible texts
Gen. 16:1-15, 131
Gen. 16:12a, 132
Gen. 21:8-20, 131
Gen. 21:10, 133
Gen. 21:17-18, 134
Gen. 21:20, 135
Gen. 25:9-17b, 135
Gen. 37:1–50:26, 136
Exod. 2:5-10, 138
Exod. 2:21-22, 138
Exod. 4:24-26, 138
Num. 12:1, 138
1 Kings 10:1-13, 139
2 Chron. 9:1-9, 139
Matt. 12:42, 140
Luke 10:42, 180 n.9
Luke 11:31, 140
Acts 8:26-40, 172
Acts 8:27b, 141
Heb. 11:1, 91
1 Pet. 3:6a, 133
Rev. 1:14, 33
Black feminism, 41–42
Black Madonna, 55–56, 172
Black nationalism, 40, 47, 56
Black power, 31, 112, 118
Black studies, 115, 179 n.13
Black theology, 169–71
Blassingame, J., 86, 102, 181 nn.7, 8, 9
Bloom, A., 32, 178 n.9
Blyden, E., 45
Briggs, S., 64, 129, 180 n.12
Brooks, E., 190 n.20; see also Higginbotham, E., 188 n.10
Brooks, G., 109–10, 186 n.42
Brown, K., 190 n.20; see also Douglas, K., 158
Burroughs, N., 16, 28, 127, 173, 188 n.11, 190 n.20

Cannon, K., 64, 107, 129, 158, 181 nn.13–14; 185 n.7, 186 n.51, 188 n.15
Carmichael, S., 49
Carpenter, D., 190 n.20
Carr-Hamilton, J., 190 n.20
Certeau, M., 81
Children, black, 45, 69–71, 75–76, 103
Children's Defense Fund, 128
Christianity, 42, 55, 66, 166–70, 173
Churches, 11–12, 14–15, 17, 24–26, 43–44, 54–56,

63–65, 74–75, 155, 159, 164–65
Circumcision, 136
Cixous, H., 99
Classism, 10, 74, 153
Collins, P., 41–42, 68–69, 150, 154, 163–64, 177 n.3, 179 n.16, 181 nn.2, 4; 189 nn.3, 5, 9, 10; 190 nn.11, 12
Cone, J., 129
Cooper, A., 21, 28, 42
Copher, C., 129
Cummings, L., 5, 7, 12, 14, 57

Davis, Angela, 181 n.6
Davis, Arthur, 185 n.10, 186 n.35
Derrida, J., 91
Diop, C., 30, 178 n.7
Douglas, K., 5–7, 9, 14–15, 16–17, 67, 147, 158; see also Brown, K., 190 n.20
Douglass, F., 45
Downing, B., 172
DuBois, W., 21, 27, 30, 32, 45–46, 60, 178 n.3

Edelman, M., 16, 128, 188 n.12
Eisenstein, Z., 186 n.53
Elaw, Z., 16, 123–25, 187 n.5
Ellison, R., 84, 182 n.9
Emecheta, B., 52, 179 n.16
Epistemology, 162–64
Ethiopian Orthodox Church, 40
Eugene, T., 158, 190 n.20
Eurocentrism, 10, 57, 59, 158, 162–63

Families, black, 22–23, 69–77, 108, 115, 135, 137, 150–51, 154, 164–65
Felder, C., 129, 188 n.18
Feminism, 53
Foote, J., 16, 123–25, 187 n.5
Frazier, E., 23, 177 n.2
Friedan, B., 54
Garvey, M., 39, 45–46, 48, 60
Gates, H., 35, 178 n.13, 182 n.10, 184 nn.18, 20
Genital mutilation, 52, 56
Genocide, 45, 77
Genovese, E., 102
Gilkes, C., 5, 7, 12–13, 21, 64, 68, 129, 177 n.2, 180 n.11, 181 n.3, 190 n.20
Giovanni, N., 16, 116, 186 n.38
Glazer, N., 31, 178 n.8
God, 15, 33, 38, 42, 55, 63–64, 66–67, 76, 81–82,

105, 122–25, 131, 133–35,
137–40, 142, 148, 153, 155
Gorgon, 37–38
Gossett, T., 29
Grant, J., 62, 158, 180 n.7
Gutman, H., 102
Guy-Sheftall, B., 118, 186 n.52

Hamer, F., 42
Hansberry, L., 108
Hardman-Cromwell, Y., 6–8,
12, 15–16, 105
Heterosexism, 67, 74, 153
Higginbotham, E., 188 n.10;
see also Brooks, E., 190 n.20
Hilliard, A., 29
Homophobia, 75–76, 152
Hood, R., 33, 178 n.12
hooks, b., 179 n.7
Howard University, 12, 26,
171–74
Hughes, L., 118, 186 n.55
Hurston, Z., 16, 110–11

Infertility, 132
Isis, 48, 52
Islam, 42, 135–36, 166–69

James, G., 30, 178 n.5
Jazz, 34–35
Jesus Christ, 33, 55, 64–65,
76, 105, 122, 140–43, 149,
153, 155
Jones, G., 81
Jones, J., 72–73, 182 n.11
Joseph, G., 116–17, 186
nn.45, 48
Judaism, 42

Karenga, R., 44–46
King, D., 21, 177 n.1
King, M., 37, 46, 48
Kundera, M., 101

Laing, R., 24
Lee, J., 14, 16, 63, 81–82, 123–
25, 180 nn.8, 10; 181 nn.15,
17, 19; 182 n.2, 187 n.5
Lesbian, lesbianism, 116, 152
Lewis, J., 116–17, 186 nn.45,
48
Lorde, A., 189 n.4

Madhubuti, H., 45
Malcolm X, 45, 48
Marriage, 72–73, 139
Marshall, P., 111, 183 n.12
Martin, C., 129
Marxism, 167
McDowell, D., 5, 8, 13, 15,
81
Mecca, 136
Misogyny, 14, 56

Mitchell, E., 128. 188 n.13
Moore, Queen Mother, 39–41
Morrison, T., 82, 96, 102,
107–8, 182 n.5, 183 n.12,
184 n.27
Moynihan Report, 23, 177 n.2
Muhammad, E., 45–46, 48
Multiculturalism, 32
Murray, P., 42

Newsome, C., 127, 188 n.9,
190 n.20
Njia, 50, 60, 167
nommo, 159
Nzingha, 56

Olsen, T., 115, 186 n.39

Parks, Rosa, 46
Patriarchy, 62–63, 66, 117
Pedagogy, 16–17, 148–55
Polygamy, 52
Poverty, 25, 67
Preaching, black women's, 16,
33, 64–66, 123–25, 128

Racism, 9–10, 28–30, 34, 37,
39, 41, 53, 67, 74, 118–19,
126, 153
Rape, 137, 184 n.19
Richardson, M., 187 n.2
Rodgers, C., 113, 185 nn.27,
28
Rogers, J., 30
Robinson, I., 190 n.20
Russell, L., 129, 188 n.15
Russell, S., 108, 115, 184 n.1,
185 nn.8, 9, 11, 12, 20, 21,
22, 24; 186 nn.34, 36, 40,
41, 44

Sanchez, S., 115
Sanctified church, 25–27
Sanders, C., 6, 8, 12, 16–17,
121, 157, 188 n.13, 190
n.20
Satiafa, 111–12, 185 nn.25, 26
Schlesinger, A., 32, 178 n.9
Schüssler Fiorenza, E., 128,
188 n.14
Sexism, 10–11, 14, 50, 53, 56,
66–68, 74–76, 110, 118–19,
126, 153
Shange, N., 82, 111, 113–14,
117, 186 n.30
Single parenting, 134
Slave narratives, 86, 99
Slavery, slaves, 27, 29, 31–33,
38, 68, 83–87, 131, 134,
136–37
Smith, A., 16, 124–25, 187
n.5

Snowden, F., 33, 178 n.11
Spencer, A., 105–6
Spirituality, 11, 160
Stetson, E., 115, 185 nn.2, 15,
16, 17; 186 n.37
Stewart, M., 16, 105–6, 122,
187 n.2
Stokes, O., 24
Styron, W., 85, 183 nn.16, 17
Sudic ideal, 159
Surrogate motherhood, 132

Tate, C., 106, 107, 114, 118,
185 nn.4, 6, 13, 14, 23, 29;
186 nn.32, 33, 40, 47, 49,
50
Theological education, 17,
147–54, 165–75
Thiam, A., 52, 179 nn.17, 18
Thurman, H., 37, 123, 173,
187 n.4
Trible, P., 128, 188 n.14
Trulear, H., 190 n.20
Truth, S., 76, 122
Tubman, H., 45, 48, 60, 122
Turner, N., 45, 48, 85

Wade-Gayles, G., 107, 117–18,
185 n.5, 186 nn.46, 53
Walker, A., 9, 15, 36–39, 42,
58, 81–82, 108–10, 114,
116, 158–61, 177 nn.1, 4;
178 n.14, 180 nn.1, 5; 181
nn.1, 20; 182 n.1, 185 n.18,
186 nn.31, 43; 189 nn.2, 4
Walker, D., 45
Walker, M., 16, 54, 84, 109,
115, 180 n.19, 186 n.38
Wallace, M., 48, 179 n.8
Washington, B., 29, 46
Washington, M., 29
Webber, T., 187 n.3
Weber, M., 27
Weems, R., 129, 158, 188
n.16
Welsh, K., 45, 179 n.1
Wheatley, P., 16, 121, 187 n.1
White, D., 71, 102, 181 n.10,
182 n.12
White supremacy, 29, 53
Williams, D., 82, 130, 158,
180 n.6, 182 n.19, 190 n.20
Williams, S., 15, 85, 87, 183
nn.12, 15; 184 n.21
Womanist theology, 147–48,
153–55
Womanism, 9–10, 36, 58, 67,
149, 151, 153, 158–59
Women's Day, 23, 27
Woodson, C., 27–28, 30

Yoruba, 168